John Newton

WOMEN OF FAITH SERIES

Amy Carmichael
Corrie ten Boom
Florence Nightingale
Gladys Aylward
Hannah Whitall Smith
Isobel Kuhn
Mary Slessor
Joni

MEN OF FAITH SERIES

Borden of Yale
Brother Andrew
C. S. Lewis
Charles Finney
Charles Spurgeon
D. L. Moody
Eric Liddell
George Muller
Hudson Taylor
Jim Elliot
John Hyde
John Newton
John Wesley
Jonathan Goforth
Martin Luther
Samuel Morris
Terry Waite
William Carey
William Booth

John and Betty Stam

John
Newton

Catherine Swift

BETHANY HOUSE PUBLISHERS
MINNEAPOLIS, MINNESOTA 55438

Originally published in England by Marshall Pickering, an imprint of HarperCollins Publishers, Ltd. under the title, *John Newton* © 1991 Catherine Swift.

Cover by Dan Thornberg,
Bethany House Publishers staff artist.

Published by Bethany House Publishers
A Ministry of Bethany Fellowship, Inc.
11300 Hampshire Avenue South
Minneapolis, Minnesota 55438

Printed in the United States of America

Library of Congress Cataloging-in-Publication Data

Swift, Catherine M.
    John Newton / Catherine Swift.
        p.   cm. — (Men of faith)
    1. Newton, John. 1725–1807. 2. Church of England—Clergy—Biography. 3. Hymn writers—England—Biography. I. Title. II. Series.
BX5199.N55S85   1994
283'.092—dc20   94–26319
[B]
ISBN 1–55661–305–9   CIP

Contents

1

London—The New City

*I*n the early eighteenth century, when John Newton was born, London was, naturally, a very different city from the one we know today. But it had also greatly changed from the London of the previous century—due entirely to the Great Fire in 1666. At that time nearly all the buildings were constructed of wood, so when fire broke out in a baker's shop in Pudding Lane, the flames quickly spread, consuming everything in their path. It took four days and nights to extinguish the inferno, by which time 13,000 houses and 87 churches, including St. Paul's Cathedral, were razed to the ground.

With vast numbers left homeless, even before the last smoldering debris was cleared away, a gigantic rebuilding project was under way. In the sixty years following that disaster, during Charles II's reign, no fewer than five different monarchs occupied the British throne. But with the exception of Charles' brother, James II, who was forced into abdication, not one had a child to succeed him. Therefore, on Queen Anne's death in 1714, the sole claimant to the British throne was a German cousin, George of Hanover. He spoke not a word of English, nor did he bother to learn it, as he lived his entire life in Germany, leaving his English ministers to rule in his absence. Fortunately, they did this so well that, by 1725, the year John Newton was born, Britain was poised on the brink of national prosperity.

The rebuilding program was continuing and London's streets and courts were now cobblestoned. Brick or stone houses replaced old, rat-infested, tinder-dry dwellings. And, in addition to forty-nine other churches, Sir Christopher Wren had designed and rebuilt the magnificent St. Paul's Cathedral.

John Newton's father, also John, was captain of a merchant ship and was often away from England for months at a time. As a child, John had been brought up in the Roman Catholic faith by Jesuits in Spain while his father was away at sea. The Jesuits were a strict order and, under the leadership of a *General*, were trained like soldiers—obeying every command without question, and they imposed this same discipline upon their students.

Although Captain Newton had later renounced Roman Catholicism for the Protestant faith, he continued to observe the Jesuit training in both his professional and private life, running his home as strictly as he captained his ship. He was quite unaffectionate toward his wife and was an extremely stern parent, treating John more like a ship's cabin boy than his own son. He was only permitted to speak when spoken to, had to stand at attention when addressed, and could sit only when given permission. Not even spontaneous laughter was allowed. It had to be stifled until the Captain—as he liked to be called—laughed first.

A tall, slender stature with swarthy coloring, coupled with his delusions of grandeur, gave Captain Newton an imperious air. Rather than captain of a small merchant ship he behaved as though he owned the vessel; instead of tenant of his small, cozy house, one could easily believe he was a titled peer with enormous wealth and lands. Colleagues, and particularly his neighbors, ridiculed him behind his back but nevertheless respected him for his good seamanship. If any man could sail a vessel out and return it safely to home port it was Captain John Newton.

The Newtons lived in the area of London that had been devastated by the Great Fire, so that their house was one of the most modern. Although small and cozy, compared with the houses of some of London's dockland inhabitants, it was considered large and extremely luxurious. It abounded with all sorts of exotic fabrics and bric-a-brac the Captain had brought back from his voyages—ornaments, trinkets, rugs, the quilt on John's bed, and the soft, colorful shawls his mother wore. All of these the child lovingly handled and, much as he loved the quiet peace of his home, he was filled with curiosity about their places of origin and wondered what it must be like to sail the Mediterranean.

Each Sunday morning, when home between voyages, the Captain took young John to a Church of England service where he would have to endure long, intoned, sleep-inducing psalms. John's mother, however, was from a Dissenter family, a sect more concerned with the goodness in man rather than with his sins, and had a stronger belief in heaven than in hell's everlasting fire.

Elizabeth Newton was a quiet, gentle little creature with sad, dark eyes set in a sweet face; her nut-brown hair always held in place by a dainty, lace cap. She rarely mixed with anyone outside her home, so no one, except her son, would have dreamed she had a sense of humor, with a delightful laugh to accompany it, and that she and John shared many private jokes.

Preferring his mother's companionship above all others, he didn't mix with children from the neighborhood. There was no compulsory education at that time so he didn't meet them at school either. However, he was more fortunate than thousands of children. Elizabeth Newton was a self-educated woman and taught her son everything she knew: reading, writing, mathematics, and poetry. When he was five years old she even introduced him to elementary Latin. Her handwriting was a work of art and, by constantly reading it, John unknowingly adopted the same beautiful style.

In her husband's absence, Elizabeth took John to her own place of worship, the Dissenter Chapel run by the well-respected Dr. David Jennings. To the child, these services were also tedious, with their meaningless prayers and boring sermons, but he loved singing the tuneful, lively hymns. In his father's church, only the choir sang and there were no melodious hymns. Those at the Dissenter Chapel were usually written by Isaac Watts, a friend of David Jennings. He'd also produced a catechism for young people, which Elizabeth used in *Jack's* religious instruction. His own chapel was in the center of London, so quite often, the chubby, rose-apple-cheeked man with flowing white hair went over to preach at the Sunday services in David's chapel.

On the short walk home, mother and son would discuss the service. How John admired a man with such music and poetry in his soul as to write "O God, Our Help in Ages Past" and "When I Survey the Wondrous Cross"; the words so simple yet saying so much. Deeply stirred by them, he declared that when he grew up he was going to be a minister. He would then assume the pose of Dr. Jennings or Isaac Watts preaching from the pulpit.

This made his mother chuckle and secretly pray he would retain his ambition. Her dearest wish was for him to attend St. Andrew's University in Fife, Scotland, where Dr. Jennings had been a student, then go on to become a minister of the chapel.

Yet in her heart she knew it would never be. Even as he talked of it she couldn't help noticing, on that walk along the street to home, how John frequently screwed up his shortsighted eyes and let his gaze stray to the tall masts of the skyline. Unwittingly, he was displaying the fact that his own little heart was torn between love of chapel and the sea; and Elizabeth knew which would be the victor.

The day would come, all too soon, when still little more than a child, he would be wrenched from her by the Captain to start a life at sea, and her dream would be shattered.

Fascinated by all the activity around the docks, John often lay awake wondering what it was like on the open sea with no sight of land for days—or weeks. How Elizabeth hated those times when, more by gesture than words, his father invited him to the docks. And trotting along behind the haughty, distinguished figure, young John, a miniature replica of his father, would be as proud as any small boy could be.

Parts of the city that had escaped the Great Fire were as deprived as ever. In the dock area at Wapping, dirt roads ran mud in rainy weather. There were mean, uncobbled streets and narrow, dark alleyways where little light penetrated. Here lived footpads and pickpockets who preyed on the more affluent parts of the city. Gin drinkers—women, and children—lay in drunken stupors on the ground. There was no sanitation of any kind and putrid, open gulleys carried all manner of filth, including sewage, down to the River Thames.

Both banks of the river were lined with gunsmiths, blacksmiths, potteries, and dye works, all emitting acrid smoke into the already densely smokey atmosphere thrown out from domestic chimneys.

On reaching the docks, while the Captain went about some business, the boy would wander around the quayside. He watched as ships' victualers and deck-officers supervised the unloading of provisions brought from the chandlers by horse and cart; candles, oil and wicks for lamps and lanterns; soap and paint alongside groceries and other foodstuffs, with all their various odors. Barrels, sacks, and crates were stacked alongside the high warehouse walls while some were being loaded onto the little bumboats plying to and from dockside to ship.

When his father joined him, they would board the longboat from his ship and be rowed out to where the vessel was riding at anchor in the Pool. There, Captain Newton would check on the loading of cargo, all sail and carpentry repairs, and other general preparation necessary for a lengthy voyage destined to last weeks or months.

John would climb up to the quarterdeck to get a better view of other ships anchored close-by, picking out their exciting names and admiring the colorful figureheads on their prows. Narrowing his eyes against the light, he would gaze along the mighty Thames, all the while breathing in the pungent odors of tar and varnish.

Watching the little bumboats scurrying about the river carrying supplies to the ships being fitted out for their next voyage, John would imagine it was he who was setting sail for the warm Mediterranean waters. Sadly, though filled with curiosity about the voyages, he was too in awe of his father to ask him about them.

As daylight was fading, they would be rowed back to Wapping Stairs which were sometimes wet and slimy. But the child, cold, tired, hungry, and usually wet, would be left to struggle up them without the aid of a fatherly hand held out to him. Once more he would fall in step behind the Captain, and with rarely a word passing between them, they would make their way to their trim, comfortable home.

At that time of day, young John would be witness to stumbling drunks, brawls, foul language, and crude, loudmouthed women with painted faces and gaudy clothes. How Elizabeth longed to protect him from all the lewd vulgarity his father happily exposed him to. She was particularly concerned about his having nightmares as he had had after seeing an executed pirate hanging from the gallows on the mudbank, awaiting the customary submersion by three high tides prior to burial.

On their arrival home, there would be a welcoming fire and a hot meal of boiled mutton, dumplings, and pease pudding followed by delicious fruit tarts. While the Captain drank a tankard of ale, John, unlike the miserable children he'd seen lying in alleys and doorways, would drink a mug of hot, sweet tea.

As she fussed around, Elizabeth, pleased to have the child safely home, would have dearly loved to hug him. But she knew it would be disapproved of by her husband and resented by the boy while under his respected father's gaze. Elizabeth always felt guilty as she watched her husband swagger off down the street heading for another voyage. For, rather than weeping as other wives did, she heaved a sigh of relief and yet, she had a great admiration for him.

From John's earliest days, his mother had never been without a cough, so he attached no importance to it. But her unnaturally bright eyes and the pink patches high on her cheekbones betrayed the presence of consumption—tuberculosis—for which there was then no cure. And whenever she lay on the sofa, clutching a Spanish shawl about her frail shoulders, John thought she was simply tired; at 29 she seemed quite an old lady to the six-year-old boy.

Elizabeth had a cousin, also named Elizabeth, and throughout their childhood they'd been so close they were more like sisters. But since Elizabeth Churchill had married a Customs Officer, George Catlett, and gone to live at Chatham in Kent, they didn't see much of each other. Young John couldn't remember ever meeting her.

Captain Newton was away on a voyage when Mrs. Catlett made one of her rare visits to London, and in the few years since they'd met she couldn't believe the change in Elizabeth. Aged beyond her years, coughing, stooped and, but for the telltale bright pink patches on her cheeks, ashen pale. With one glance she decided her cousin must get right away from London's smoke and dirt and return with her to the clean air of Kent's hop fields, orchards, and the sea. Acting immediately, she began packing Elizabeth's clothes and making ready to close the house up. She was at a loss, though, what to do with John. His mother was dreadfully ill, and if Elizabeth couldn't nurse her back to health she didn't want him to see her steadily getting worse. She confided her problem to Dr. Jennings, who suggested John should be left behind, and arranged for some friends to take him into their home until Elizabeth recovered.

John stood in silent bewilderment as his frail mother was helped aboard a hackney carriage. Then he tearfully watched it clatter down the street, heading for London Bridge to cross the river, then continue across the city to where they would take the stage-wagon for Chatham.

With his mother gone and his father heaven knew where—or if he were still alive—John felt totally isolated. Even if his father survived storm, tempest, and pirates, or any other hazard encountered by mariners, it could be months before he returned. Still, he consoled himself that before then his mother would be fully recovered and back in London. In any case, she'd promised to be home for his seventh birthday in July.

Alas, within weeks of her departure for the south coast and the pure air that was hopefully going to restore her to health, Elizabeth Newton died at the age of thirty.

2

A Changed Life

John's guardian told him as gently as possible of his mother's death, then took him around to his home where they tied a black crepe ribbon on the doorknocker to show it was a house of mourning. Afterwards, he was dressed in somber black clothes for the duration of the mourning period—about a year.

Now that he'd lost his dearest companion, there was only one person he could turn to for consolation—David Jennings. He was so kind and understanding, John was even more determined that when he grew up he would fulfill his mother's wish and go into the church.

As the months passed by, though, and he missed her more and more, he found himself longing for his father, too. And with those longings, his love for the sea and interest in all things maritime started to overwhelm him. They grew so strong that neither prayers nor hymns gave him any comfort.

Captain Newton arrived home in the following spring of 1733. Of course, he'd always known about Elizabeth's illness, but the sea being his livelihood, he'd had to go about his duties. However, whether

or not her death came as a shock, he displayed absolutely no grief nor allowed John to show any or
even speak of her.

Without bothering to observe the usual mourning period, within a couple of weeks, he announced
that he was going to remarry and introduced John
to Thomasin, his future stepmother. It all happened
so quickly John had barely recovered from his father's homecoming when he found himself packed up
in a cart alongside all the Newton household effects. With the Captain and his new wife—a total
stranger—he was heading for Avely in Essex, about
fifteen miles from London, where they were going
to live with Thomasin's father on his farm.

Thomasin was a number of years younger than
the Captain. She'd had no experience with children
and didn't know how to handle a ready-made,
seven-and-a-half-year-old son, so John was largely
ignored. From the time Mrs. Newton died, John had
deliberately avoided thinking of Elizabeth Catlett.
After all, it was she who had taken his mother away
from him with the promise she would be home for
his seventh birthday.

Elizabeth Catlett, on the other hand, had promised her cousin she would help care for young John.
Assuming that, on arriving home, Captain Newton
would travel to Kent to learn the details of his wife's
death, she'd considered asking him to let John go
and live with her while he was at sea. That way, she
could really keep her promise to her cousin as he
would be brought up like one of her own children—
Polly, aged three, Elizabeth, one year old, and baby
John.

But neither John nor his father arrived at her

door. Instead, she was horrified to hear the Captain had remarried. Now she couldn't supervise John's welfare, but she consoled herself that at least he'd moved into a good home and a respected family.

John was left very much to himself but he liked his new environment. Scampering around fields and leafy lanes and fishing in clear streams was sheer delight to the town child. As was discovering all the different crops and strange farm animals he'd only heard of or read about in books. Tree climbing was another previously unknown pleasure. Precariously balancing in their branches, he could see right out over the Essex marshes to where tall ships were making their way to a mooring at Long Reach, a three-mile stretch of the Thames. He couldn't actually see the water, so the ships appeared to be sailing right through luscious green meadowland. Still, he knew they weren't and his memories would drift back with the river toward London, to his home and all the love and laughter he'd shared with his mother. But he was never allowed to speak of such times to his father.

When it came time to go back to sea, neither Thomasin nor her father wanted John around the place, so Captain Newton placed him in a nearby boarding school. This was a small establishment situated in the principal's own home and consisted of only one classroom. It had no more than a dozen pupils whose ages ranged from infancy to teens, with all their varying standards of intellect and stages of development. Surprisingly, John quickly adapted to the company of other children, something that came about through a common cause.

In those days, schools could be set up and run by

anyone, without qualifications, and there was no authority or supervision from outside except the students' parents. This school was run by a sadistic, ignorant headmaster who believed the way to impart education was by thrashing pupils with the cane or birch. Under his authority, boys became so cowed they were afraid to answer the simplest question for fear of being wrong. Consequently, such behavior resulted in further beatings.

Their days were relentless hours of study with no playtime or games. Sunday was the only day they had a break from lessons and then they attended church or chapel two or three times. Their only holidays were at Easter and Christmas, when they were given a couple of days off. And they were lonely times for John as none of his school chums lived close-by. His only pleasures were to be found on the farm or perched high in a tree gazing out toward the shipping on the distant river.

Despite their indifference, Thomasin Newton and her father were good people at heart who ensured the boy was well fed and warmly clothed. He was free to explore the farm at will, even learning horse-riding. But, although, in their own minds, they were doing their best for him, there was no warmth in their relationship and all three remained strangers.

Two years after starting school, when John was nine years old, a younger teacher joined the staff who immediately realized how intimidated the children were. With a different approach he soon had them learning without fear, and in John Newton he saw a great potential, particularly regarding Latin. In a short time, he had learned so much he was reading the "classics." This made him look ahead to a time when he might, after all, fulfill his mother's wishes and go on to the University in Scotland. For the first time since Elizabeth died, John found a degree of happiness again. But it was to last a mere two years.

When the boy was ten-and-a-half, Thomasin gave birth to his half brother, William. This joyous event should have brought them all closer as a family but, on the contrary, as Thomasin and her aging father naturally doted on the new arrival, John was completely rejected.

A few weeks later, when his father returned from his latest voyage, he seemed quite unmoved by the tiny infant and, as usual, scarcely noticed John's existence. The comparison between the baby's age and that of his older son must have affected him in some way, though. He'd always intended that John should follow the Newton family tradition and take up a life at sea. So when the Captain was ready to set off again, he suddenly declared that John should leave school and sail with him.

Living at Avely in Essex meant that rather than journey into London, the Captain now joined his ship at Long Reach. So it was from there, on July 24, 1736, John Newton's eleventh birthday, that he stepped aboard for his first voyage.

Although John was familiar with the ship, it was the first time he'd stood under billowing sails, which he soon learned to call sheets. As the order was given to weigh anchor and he was caught up in the general commotion of casting off, the exhilaration set the boy's heart pounding, fit to burst. At last, he was embarking on the experience he'd craved throughout his young life.

The Captain had enough compassion—or personal pride—to keep the boy to himself rather than fling him among a mob of rough seamen. John slept in his father's cabin and, instead of a diet of stale water and hard tack—a coarse, indigestible, tasteless biscuit—he dined on the best fare in the wardroom with the captain and officers. All the same, to allay any accusations of favoritism, John Newton treated his son more harshly than his crew.

However, John set about his chores with never a grumble and was quick to master shipping terms that were hitherto a complete mystery. He'd been at sea some days when someone, to his immense satisfaction, pointed out that he'd escaped the dreaded seasickness he'd been warned about and must therefore be "a natural sailor." On discovering that the ship's doctor was, in fact, the *cook*, he was glad he felt fit and hoped he would never need medical attention.

Despite the distance put between himself and the men, John soon grew accustomed to their crude manners. Uncouth ways and foul language, previously gone unnoticed by the small city boy, were all absorbed into his developing mind.

Each Sunday the Captain held morning services on deck. Attendance was compulsory as some crew members were reluctant to take part. The proceedings were a world away from the quiet reverence and heartfelt joy of Dr. Jennings' chapel and the hymns of Isaac Watts. Throughout the prayers and hymns, rather than join in, the men were inclined to snicker and make crass remarks. It seemed they thought it manly to scoff at God.

Elizabeth had taught her son to respect others' opinions, for even his own father attended a different place of worship than his wife. But for John, it was impossible to find anything in his heart for these people but utter contempt.

Approaching the Strait of Gibraltar, which had been in Britain's possession for a mere 32 years, John marveled at the small, seemingly barren Rock, now securing shipping in and out of the Mediterranean Sea. He wondered at the Barbary apes, descendants of the macaque monkeys that once roamed Europe and now lived solely on the Rock.

Once safely through the Strait, his mind turned to the scourge of the Mediterranean that hailed from North African ports—the notorious Barbary pirates. These outlaws roamed the five Mediterranean Seas, capturing ships and their crews to hold for ransom or sell into slavery. They'd once hunted the seas in oared galleys, which gave their prey time to escape. But by the eighteenth century, they'd discovered the benefit of sail, and their modern vessels, the xebecs, could close in on a vessel in a fraction of the time. Though filled with terror, John was always fascinated by horror stories of the pirates exploits, which he heard recounted below decks.

The Mediterranean trade covered the whole of Italy, Spain, Greece, and North Africa. Wool was Britain's chief export but there were also cargos of flour and wheat. On return voyages the holds would be crammed with such diverse commodities as silk, fruit, gold, silver, and soap. There were also spices from Arabia bought overland to North Africa and, though very expensive, there was always a market for them as they were essential ingredients for preserving and improving the taste of food.

Coastal navigation was simple, since the Mediterranean was almost tideless, and because it was August when they reached there, John reveled in the hot, semitropical climate. Autumn and winter present the greatest hazards on the sea, when the North wind blows up terrible storms. However, on his first voyage, John encountered nothing but calm seas and arrived back in England in spring.

Apart from the bad influences on board, John learned a lot about seamanship and all thoughts of being a church minister or chapel preacher were pushed from his mind.

3

Further Changes

Almost twelve, in his nine months' absence from England, John had unwittingly matured from childhood to the very brink of manhood. No longer did he want to scamper over fields, leap streams or fish for tadpoles. He wanted excitement, adventure, and couldn't wait for the next voyage. But when the time came, Captain Newton decided against taking him and John was bitterly disappointed.

Now he was no longer at school, and with Thomasin never bothering to supervise him, he was left to his own devices. Still fascinated by some of the crew's antics, he went in search of their kind and found them in a pack of wild village lads whose pastimes included plundering orchards or stowing away on farm carts for a ride to Long Reach to watch cruel cock fights.

From sheer mischief, ignoring the dangers of its broken windows, rotting stairs and floorboards, the boys went exploring Belhus, a derelict mansion house just outside Avely. When this bored them they turned to poaching game on the grounds. One day the gamekeeper caught them and they were fortunate to be given a beating—*fortunate* because in those days, even for a twelve-year-old, the penalty for poaching was prison, hanging, or deportation.

A few days later, when riding his horse too hard along a very narrow leafy lane, it stumbled, throwing John into a hedge. Angrily berating the animal, he sprang to his feet to see that he'd narrowly missed a spiked branch that would surely have gone through his eye and straight into his brain. Fear replaced his fury, and he wondered why he had escaped the real penalty for poaching and now missed death by inches.

Those incidents made John recall his mother warning him of the Day of Judgment, and for the next few months he repented and turned to prayer and reading the Bible. But eventually his abstinence from mischievous activities made him restless, so he decided a suitable penance had been completed and he returned to vandalism.

Within the year his father took him to sea again, but he was left ashore for the next voyage and again took up with the village ruffians. No sooner had he rejoined them when another, more terrifying incident occurred. A three-masted warship was moored in Long Reach, its magnificent rigging clearly visible from three miles away at Avely. John longed to go and see it for three reasons: Coming from a family of mariners and having some experience himself, he was naturally curious. He also wanted to laud his knowledge over his ignorant rustic friends who wouldn't know a mainsail from a mizzen mast or a lantern from a spanker. Furthermore, he'd heard such disturbing tales about the Royal Navy, he wanted to see for himself if they were true. Did sailors work under constant use of the rope and cane? Were there really some who weren't there of their own free will but had been captured by press gangs and imprisoned on board?

On a Friday evening, John walked over to Purfleet jetty and asked a waterman what were the chances of he and his friends getting a closer look at the huge man-of-war. Recognizing Captain Newton's son, the man offered to row them out there himself on Sunday afternoon.

How John gloated at his importance when he reported this to the village lads, but when Sunday came, every obstacle stood in his path. The sermon in church dragged on and on, then, back at the farm, Thomasin's father ate his dinner infuriatingly slow and John wasn't permitted to leave the table until he'd finished.

At last he was free and he whipped his horse the three miles to Long Reach, only to arrive in time to see the boat leaving the jetty with his friends in it, all waving and jeering. He was about to turn and leave, when suddenly the boat keeled over, pitching all its occupants into the water, drowning the waterman and several of the village lads.

This shocked John so much that at their funerals he seemed struck dumb and kept asking himself why had he been spared—again. From then on he tended to keep to himself, musing over the mysterious events and atoning with prayer for all he'd done. Then after a while he grew restless again and wandered into the village, looking for new adventure.

When John was fourteen, his life suddenly

changed again. With time, Thomasin had grown
quite fond of John, especially as he obviously cared
for his small half brother, William. Captain Newton's attitude toward him had improved too and he
planned to make provision for the boy's future.
Comparing John's seamanship with his own high
standards, he was confident the boy would never be
successful in that sphere. Instead, he took him to
Alicante in Spain, to get him apprenticed as a clerk
to an English merchant he knew. On his return to
England, after learning the trade, John could go on
to make a fortune.

John had no choice in this, and within weeks he
found himself living in a foreign country, among
strangers, and learning a trade he knew nothing
about and had no interest in.

From Spain, the Captain sailed on to continue
trading in northeast Italy and all across the east
Mediterranean. Eighteen months later, on his way
home, he put in at Alicante to check on his son's progress, only to find the distraught merchant eager to
hand his apprentice back to his father.

Although young John Newton was a cheerful
lad, he constantly daydreamed. Thoroughly bored
with his work, he couldn't concentrate on his ledg-
ers for more than a few minutes at a time and had
been downright obtuse, refusing to learn anything.
His young colleagues thought he was strange, for,
although he was as full of fun and high spirits as
the rest, all his spare time was spent poring over
religious books.

Surprisingly, the Captain neither showed anger
nor offered criticism but simply took him on board
and set off to complete his voyage, calling at various

channel ports on the way. One of them was Middleberg in Holland, where John made a discovery that changed his whole concept of God.

Being in awe of their Captain, officers and men on board were reluctant to befriend his son, so in port, while the rest went ashore in groups, John went off alone to explore the town. For over a year he'd lived in Spain. Now he was surrounded by people speaking the Dutch language. Passing an old junk shop, despite his nearsightedness, his eye caught sight of a small book whose English title stood out boldly from the rest of the stock. In search of some tangible, familiar object he walked in to the shop, picked up the book, and glimpsed through its contents. It was Volume II of the Third Earl of Shaftsbury's *Characteristics*, written in 1712.

Shaftsbury was a deist—sometimes called Freethinkers—one who believes in a Supreme Being yet doesn't feel the compulsion to follow any religious dogma. Immediately John was intrigued and, handing over a few coins to the proprietor, he bought it and returned to the ship. Opening the faded book he casually flipped through the pages until he came across a section called "The Moralists—A Philosophical Rhapsody," which seemed particularly interesting, and he settled down to read it.

John's youthful interpretation of its content was that the Bible was too generalized. What is right or wrong for one person doesn't necessarily apply to the next. Man must decide for himself what his individual moral standard must be. Naturally, this gave license to reject whatever was inconvenient or difficult to uphold, leaving one free to accept as honorable that which suited him best.

He was absolutely fascinated by these ideas and spent every spare minute of the Channel-crossing absorbed in the book and, before reaching England, he could quote the page number of any particular paragraph. Back in Avely after his lengthy absence, instead of looking up his village companions, he spent the entire summer reading the same book over and over, until he knew almost every page word for word.

Suddenly, everything he'd learned from his mother—Isaac Watts' Catechism, and his beautiful hymns about Jesus Christ: *The Young Prince of Glory, O God, Our Help in Ages Past*—appeared to be mere fable and folklore. Shaftsbury's book had freed the young Newton from all obligation to God.

Shortly before that last voyage, Captain Newton had announced his impending retirement from the sea as he'd been offered a post with the Royal Africa Company. This organization was set up to give British merchants the sole right to trade in slaves on the understanding they would supply 3,000 African slaves annually to the West Indian plantations. Nonmembers could only buy and sell slaves on condition they paid ten percent of their profits to the Company.

This appointment meant Captain Newton, Thomasin, and their small son, William, would be moving to London where they had bought an elegant townhouse. Still not knowing what to do with his older, wayward son, the Captain contacted yet another friend and asked if he would take John on as Third Mate for his next voyage to the Mediterranean. This would give the lad an opportunity to prove his seamanship in his own right rather than under his father's surveillance.

But just as in Alicante, the captain couldn't wait to rid himself of the troublesome youth and told Captain Newton his son was an idler and a dreamer. He would never be any good as a sailor, much less earn the respect his father did. He couldn't be relied upon to perform his duties and was, therefore, a dangerous liability to his fellow seamen.

Desperate to find something suitable, Captain Newton then approached Joseph Manesty, a Liverpool shipowner with shares in Jamaican sugar plantations. The proposition he put to him would thrust John into an entirely different career from anything previously considered.

At seventeen, he was being sent to Jamaica in the West Indies to work as an overseer of slaves on one of Manesty's plantations. He would live like a king, be waited on hand and foot by slaves, and wield more power than in all his wildest daydreams. There were good opportunities for young men out there, too. With early promotion to management, he could soon become independent, start his own plantation, and make a fortune by the time he reached thirty.

At the promise of earning a fortune, John leaped at the chance while his father looked even further ahead. Someday his successful son would return to England, perhaps go into Parliament and become one of the landed gentry, thus fulfilling his father's own delusions of grandeur.

There were just two weeks to prepare for his new life, which would take him first to Liverpool in the northwest of England, where he would board ship for Jamaica. The captain spared nothing to fit John out, providing him with fine luggage and an expensive wardrobe of clothes to suit every working and social occasion on the island.

With less than a week before his departure, John was annoyed when his father asked him to ride into Kent to attend to some urgent business in Maidstone. It was a bitterly cold winter and John was reluctant to go, but considering what his father was doing for him he couldn't refuse.

Then, before going to Kent, a letter arrived for him from Elizabeth Catlett. She'd never forgotten the pathetic little figure sadly waving farewell to his mother, little realizing it was his final goodbye to her. Elizabeth had often regretted her decision not to take John in, even though, if she had, his father would have claimed him upon his return from the sea.

Nevertheless, through discreet enquiries from various sources, she'd always managed to follow John's progress throughout his childhood. After he started going to sea with his father she'd lost track of him for a while. But now, knowing he was back in England, and seventeen years old, she assumed he was more or less independent of the Captain and therefore decided to write to him. It was a simple letter asking of his welfare and saying she would be delighted to see him if ever he was in Kent.

It was sheer coincidence that he was being sent into that very county on business for his father, and to a place that would take him a mere half mile from her home. The Captain gave John leave to visit the Catletts, but John wasn't really interested in meeting Elizabeth. He'd always associated her name with the loss of his mother and, furthermore, he didn't want to visit the house where she had been ill and died.

On an exceptionally cold day, the twelfth of December, he rode out to Maidstone. By late afternoon, when his business was completed, he was frozen with cold, tired, hungry, and thoroughly miserable. It was reminiscent of his childhood visits to his father's ship and the wharves, and his mind turned briefly to the warm, loving welcome his mother always gave him. He faced a thirty-mile ride back to London and couldn't hope to be there before the early hours of the following day. So that, coupled with the hope of getting warm and having something to eat, prompted him to turn off the main road and make his way along an ice-rutted lane to the Catlett's home; a large, detached house surrounded by neat gardens.

Dismounting his horse, he made his way through the gates and walked along the short drive toward the door. Even at that stage he hesitated, wondering if he should turn and leave rather than risk opening up old wounds. He wasn't sure if he could enter the house let alone force himself to be sociable to its mistress. For a couple of minutes he stamped his feet and slapped his arms, then unaware of the great step he was about to take, he moved forward, knocked on the door with his clenched fist and waited.

4

Rebellion

*I*n answer to his loud rapping, the door was opened by whom he assumed to be the parlor-maid. Then Elizabeth Catlett, whom he remembered instantly, appeared, and from her demeanor he realized he had been wrong; the "parlor-maid" was Mrs. Catlett's daughter.

As John bore the familiar features of her dear cousin, Elizabeth Newton, it only took Mrs. Catlett one glance to recognize the young man. Running forward she drew him into the hall and embraced him warmly, then called for a groom to feed, water, and stable his horse.

John was ushered into a cozy living room where a group of laughing children was gathered around a man seated in front of a roaring fire. Elizabeth introduced him as her husband, George, and they both suggested he call them aunt and uncle. This was followed by introductions to the children. The girl who had opened the door to him was fourteen-year-old Mary—known affectionately as Polly. Next came twelve-year-old Elizabeth; Jack, eleven; Sarah, four; two-year-old Susannah, and baby George, asleep in his cradle.

The little ones were impressed by this previously unknown, well-traveled cousin with a host of tales to tell. But of all the family, though she wasn't a particularly pretty girl, it was Polly who caught his attention.

As they all sat around the table eating and later by the fire talking, the other children, who already obviously adored him, gazed into his eyes. But as he recounted his life and adventures since his mother died, John's eyes constantly wandered in Polly's direction.

He was given a bed for the night, and next morning, at breakfast, Elizabeth and George said they were so happy to have him under their roof at last, he was welcome to stay for as long as he wanted. And, irresponsibly, John accepted the invitation. He omitted to tell them he'd gone to Kent on business and not simply to visit them. Nor did he tell them that, within two days, he was due to leave for Liverpool from where he would sail to the West Indies to take up a career.

Even on such short acquaintance, John knew he was in love with Polly. Lying in bed in the dark, he secretly made up his mind that in Jamaica he would work hard, quickly amass a huge fortune, then return and claim her for his bride. It didn't occur to him that she wouldn't want to marry him or that she might, by then, be married to someone else.

There was one drawback to amassing that fortune though; John couldn't bear to tear himself away from Polly to go to Jamaica in the first place.

Days passed, and with them the day on which he should have sailed for Jamaica. Christmas was drawing near, and with the excitement of preparation he had found it impossible to leave. He'd never known such merrymaking—children collecting masses of evergreens and dragging in enormous yule logs; Aunt Elizabeth making plum puddings and inviting everyone to give a stir; Polly helping to make the yule cake.

On Christmas Eve, the children plucked an enormous goose; then, before bedtime, Polly led carol singing in the sweetest, clearest voice John had ever heard. In chapel on Christmas morning, he sat next to Polly, who wore a new dress. Home again, everyone exchanged small gifts amid squeals of delight and laughter. In the evening, with candles flickering on the holly and mistletoe boughs, Polly read poetry to her adoring little brothers and sisters.

Filled from good food, wine, and forever eating nuts and crystallized fruits, John was still exhausted when the New Year came around. However, he couldn't impose on his Aunt Elizabeth and Uncle George forever. And only now did he begin worrying about his father's wrath when he returned to London. He hadn't dared write to him explaining his absence and he couldn't bring himself to concoct a string of lies.

Meanwhile, the Captain, Thomasin, and little William were desperately worried, wondering whatever had happened to him. Had he been press-ganged into the Royal Navy? Or even worse, waylaid by highwaymen, murdered and his body left lying in some concealed place?

It was almost a month before John finally left Chatham, by which time the ship bound for Jamaica had been at sea two weeks. When he heard his story, Captain Newton was furious but so relieved that he'd come to no harm, he soon calmed down. Nevertheless, he felt John should have some sort of punishment. Knowing of a merchantman that was due to leave for a year's voyage to the Levant—east Mediterranean—he arranged for John to sail on her as a common sailor, without rank.

Rather than resent this, John was relieved. A year was a long time to wait before he saw Polly again, but it was better than a decade or more in Jamaica.

The voyage turned out to be different from any previous one. Before he'd either been the son of the ship's captain or had his own rank. Now, far from spending hours poring over his treasured book, *Characteristics*, he was scrubbing decks, scrambling up rat-lines, and mending coarse, canvas sails that rubbed his fingers so raw, they bled. No longer sharing a comfortable cabin, he slept with the rest of the crew and lived on hardtack. Very soon he was swearing, smoking a clay pipe, and delighting in telling lewd tales.

At the Sabbath service he fell in with the very types who had disgusted him when he first sailed as a child of eleven. Now he too joined in the scoffing and snide remarks behind the captain's back. Ashore he frequented taverns with his companions and, though he didn't drink much himself, he enjoyed persuading others to get drunk.

Still, in quiet moments, his thoughts turned to the sweet smile of Polly Catlett with her dimples. Her impish laughter, in contrast to her shyness,

echoed in his ears and he counted the weeks till his
return.

One night while sailing down the Adriatic from
Venice in northeast Italy, John had a strange experience. It didn't seem to have any significance at
the time, but it stayed with him for the rest of his
life. Having come off watch some hours earlier, by
the time the ship was passing through the Strait of
Otranto, he was fast asleep when he had a most pe-
culiar dream. In it he was back in the first hour of
his watch in port late at night. For some days they'd
been becalmed, but the still silence that suddenly
enveloped him was uncanny. No sounds from the
town; no creaking timbers on board. The rest of the
watch could neither be seen nor heard and he began
to feel nervous.

Acting on instinct, he turned to see a figure had
stealthily approached and was standing on the
quay within touching distance of him. Quickly re-
gaining his composure, John was about to chal-
lenge him when the man smiled and held his hand
out toward him. In his palm rested a gold ring set
with a diamond, its facets dancing and glinting in
the half-light. He urged John to take it, to keep it,
and guard it carefully, thus securing himself a
happy and fruitful life. But he warned that if he
ever lost it or gave it away he would incur nothing
but strife and sadness.

Thanking him profusely, John put the ring on
his finger and it fit perfectly. He turned to thank the
stranger once more—but he'd vanished, leaving
John to continue his vigil. From time to time he
glanced at his gift and smiled at the promise it carried. Deep in thought, he started as the half-hour

watch bell shattered the silence. At the dying tones he saw the donor return and feared he was coming to reclaim his gift. But as he focused his near-sighted eyes on him, he saw it was a different man dressed in identical clothing. When he admired the ring, John told him how he'd come by it and of the happiness it guaranteed. The man exploded with laughter and told him he was stupid and naive. How could a grown man believe in such superstitious nonsense?

At first, John defended himself but gradually the stranger's taunting wore him down until he agreed the idea was stupid. "Throw it away. Toss it overboard," the man urged. And with his laughter pounding in his ears, John wrenched the ring from his finger and flung it from him.

In an instant, a volcano on the far horizon erupted with a roar and orange flames belched into the night sky. Immediately, the stranger stopped laughing. In an accusing voice he declared that all of God's mercy and love had been encapsulated in that ring, "Yet you willingly threw it away." He went on to threaten John that all the fires of hell awaited him and with that he turned and fled into the night. John was aghast at what he'd done and at how easily he'd been fooled.

Then, the first man returned and asked to see the ring. When he saw John shaking with terror he asked why and John told him. "If it is returned to you, will you be wiser in the future and not heed temptation?" When John assured him he would, the man leaped into the water and resurfaced with the ring. But just as he was about to hand it over he changed his mind and quickly withdrew it. "If you

have it, you will soon forget your folly and repeat it.
I will hold the ring for you and bring it whenever
you need it."

John awoke with a start from his nightmare and
pondered on it all through the night. For the rest of
the voyage across the Mediterranean to Spain and
then home he was a changed man. No curse or lewd
song passed his lips and he became the most atten-
tive crew member at Sabbath services.

However, back in England at the end of the year,
to his father and Thomasin he was a noticeably
changed person in other ways. He was eighteen, yet
he hadn't matured so much as coarsened, and the
Captain feared his "punishment" had done more
harm than good. Nevertheless, he already had urgent plans for John to sail again.

In 1740, when the German Emperor Charles VI
died, his daughter, Maria Theresa, inherited Germany and Austria. There were many, though, who
rejected a female line of succession; some who
claimed the throne for themselves. The most likely
to succeed with his claim was Philip V of Spain, an
ally of France, and this was something England
couldn't afford to let happen. With her old enemy
Spain allied to another old adversary, France, their
combined power—lying just across the Channel—
could prove disastrous for Britain, so she sided with
Maria Theresa and war became imminent between
France and England. Already the French navy was
ready to sail and England was busily preparing her
ships for a counterattack.

Other than junior officers straight from Naval
college, men weren't eager to join the Royal Navy
because of the hard life and rigorous rules. Also,

compared with the Merchant Navy, they were paid a pittance—usually only at the *end* of a voyage—and all too often in the form of vouchers that could only be used in London. With England on the brink of war, crews were desperately needed and all young men lived in fear of the press-gangs.

Sometimes pressings were made at sea when any passing merchant vessel could be boarded and the required number of men taken. But more often than not they were taken while on dry land.

Armed with cutlasses and cudgels, sailors and officers could go ashore and *legally* kidnap any able-bodied man they met on the street. Family or friends were powerless to prevent it as he was often whisked away without anyone ever knowing. Occasionally, if a man was seized while among a group of other men, it resulted in a big street fight. But as the gang was acting within the law, even the men who intervened were also likely to be abducted or, if unsuitable, severely beaten for interfering.

Press-gangs lurked in dark alleys, waiting to waylay unsuspecting passersby, or they toured taverns and inns where accomplices slipped drugs into ale, thus rendering drinkers unconscious. On awaking, they found themselves bound hand and foot in chains on board a ship's tender where they could be confined for weeks while awaiting the arrival of more unfortunates. When the required number was reached, the little boat would move out to the mother vessel, which then sailed for foreign parts for up to years at a time.

To prevent such a fate befalling John, his father had managed to get him an officer's post on a merchant ship due to sail the week after Christmas.

He'd always wanted John to be a sailor but not in a fighting ship. There were hazards enough at sea without naval battles, so he urged him to claim his officer's certificate quickly to safeguard himself.

John's only thoughts, though, were of Polly, and he intended hastening to Kent to see her. The Captain agreed but warned him to be on a constant lookout for press-gangs, especially around the busy dockyards and dark streets of Chatham.

When John arrived at the Catlett's home a few days before Christmas, they were overjoyed to see him. Once again he was caught up in the excitement and preparation for the coming festivities. His happiness at being with Polly again made him forget his nightmare about the ring and the warning it had given him. So, once more, he failed to tell them he was due to sail within a few days' time.

By the third week of January, the Captain feared he'd been press-ganged. But when John got back to London, his father felt no relief at seeing no harm had come to him. In a rage, he threatened to turn him from the house until Thomasin, who had recently been delivered of her second child, pleaded for him and he relented. This was on condition he got a place on any ship and left as soon as possible.

Because of foul weather all sailings had been delayed, so there were more ships than usual anchored in the Pool of London, but John couldn't find an officer's berth on any. Two weeks later, the Newtons were going down to Avely to show the new baby to Thomasin's father and, to keep an eye on him, the Captain insisted John go with them.

5

Press-Ganged

*B*ack in Avely, John wandered around, recalling his many childhood escapades. But as his wanderings took him farther from the farm, he could see Purfleet where a ferry crossed over to Kent and his thoughts turned to Polly. Driven by impetuosity, he raced down the fields, leaped aboard the ferry and gazed across the short stretch of water to where he would soon be landing and striding out along the Dover Road toward Chatham.

But within minutes of stepping ashore, he fell straight into the clutches of an armed press-gang. By his bearing, they recognized at once that he was a sailor. He protested that they couldn't touch him because he was an *officer*. But, of course, he had no certificate of proof nor could he confess to letting his ship sail without him. The Royal Navy had no sympathy for deserters, not even from the merchant fleet.

Roughly he was pushed along an alleyway and thrown into a dingy outhouse behind an inn. He was soon joined by nine more men, all bewailing their fate and pleading exemption for various reasons, but John seemed to be the only one with a legitimate argument.

When he'd somehow convinced them that his father was a retired sea captain, currently employed by the Royal Africa Company, he was allowed to write him a note, which a young boy delivered to Avely in return for a few coins. Once he'd received the letter, John had no doubt his father would hasten to his rescue so he settled down to wait.

It was early evening before he heard the familiar voice speaking to the lieutenant in charge of the press-gang, and he got to his feet, expecting to be released in minutes. But after a while, he noticed their voices were raised. Eventually the door opened and Captain Newton came into the room looking very grave. Taking John by the shoulders he explained there would be no concessions. On discovering that he'd sailed many times with his father, the lieutenant assumed John was an expert seaman, the sort they needed.

Furthermore, shots had been fired, heralding that France had begun her attack. To take his son away now, even if he could, would look like an act of cowardice so the Captain said a poignant "farewell" and left.

Next morning the prisoners were marched under escort to board the *Betsy*, tender to the *HMS Harwich*, a fourth-rate—50-guns—man-of-war needing to make up a contingent of 350. The ten captives were hurriedly pushed below decks into a dark hold, which was then battened down to prevent anyone escaping overboard before they'd been *impressed* into the Royal Navy. Escape after that would amount to desertion which, at best, incurred a severe flogging and, at worst, being hanged from the yardarm.

The hold was already overcrowded with men, some of whom had been there for four weeks. Over the next few days they were tossed about on the *Betsy* while awaiting other men to join them. At last, on the fourth day, they were rowed out to the *HMS Harwich*.

Most of the men were terrified as they were forced to climb the madly swinging rope-ladders up to the deck, but John clambered up with ease. Once on board, they were ordered to strip for a medical examination. After dressing they had to run at the double to meet their captain. Philip Carteret was a well-educated man with a compassionate nature. And, unlike Captain Newton with his pathetic delusions of grandeur, he came from a high-ranking family; his uncle was the King's Secretary of State.

Closely questioning the pressed men, Captain Carteret decided that, due to their experience and general demeanor, three of them should be impressed as Able Seamen rather than Ordinary, and John Newton was one of the three.

After all preparations were completed, the *HMS Harwich* finally sailed on March 8, 1744, and Able Seaman Newton was introduced to a much harder regime than anything he'd known as Ordinary Seaman in the Merchant Navy.

Built only two years previous, the *HMS Harwich* was a modern, rather small vessel, no more than 140 feet in length with a beam of 40 feet. Conditions below decks were awful. It was hot and airless and because of low headroom, everybody walked about stooped, which put a terrible strain on their backs. For the first time, John was sleeping in a hammock, slung only inches apart from its neighbor. All around him was the stench of stale breath and sweaty bodies, and seasickness was rife. Their meager food was often rancid and inedible.

Of the 350 men aboard, the 300 below decks were all pressed men. Not all were taken in the same manner as John Newton, though—a few were trade apprentices who had displeased their masters; others were wayward sons who had been handed over by their fathers for being beyond parental control. The majority were quite acceptable to John but some—violent convicts who had volunteered in order to escape the hangman or transportation to the colonies—were the worst characters he had ever known. He was so revolted, he determined to show he wasn't one of them but a well brought up, Christian son of respected parents.

One of the first rules to observe in the Royal Navy was the custom of saluting the quarterdeck each time one passed it. This originated in the days of the old galleons when a crucifix hung there, and any landlubber who didn't quickly learn to remember this rule felt the lash of a cane.

Orders were usually accompanied by a lash anyway, either from the Master at Arms' cane or a rope wielded by the Bosun or Mate. Scrambling up the rigging was a hazardous feat as it was always executed in double-quick time. This avoided the feel of the lash for tardiness on descent, but far from helping the situation, it often incurred accidents.

The reasoning behind all this was that men wouldn't be hardened and conditioned for battle if they weren't already accustomed to brutal treatment from their own masters. They were driven to exhaustion and, in effect, were nothing more than slaves.

Ironically though, because of their captain, compared to others the men were spared a particularly harsh existence. It wasn't unknown in other ships for pressed men to hurl themselves to their death into the ocean from the yardarm rather than face life on board.

John had expected they would put to sea within days of the ship becoming fully manned but a month later, due to appalling weather, they were still at anchor in the River Medway at Sheerness, Kent.

Despite the elements, ships had to be maintained, and the crew was forced, under threat of whip or cane, to scrape the ship's sides. After the scraping they had to paint the timbers with tallow—animal fat and resin—a residue of turpentine to preserve them from Toredo worm. This parasite originated in tropical waters but had been transported on ships' keels to every ocean in the world. Without the timbers being treated, the worms would eat their way into the hull until it was a mass of perforations resembling a sieve, and sink the ship.

It was snowing and high winds buffeted the workers against the ship's hull, threatening to dislodge them from the rope cradles supporting them. Numbed hands and feet made it almost impossible to work.

On April 3, Captain Carteret called for all hands on deck to tell them England had declared war on

France. Two days later, John was ordered to the captain's cabin. As no Able Seaman was ever ordered thus unless he'd committed a very serious offense, he was shaking with trepidation. But to his relief it was to discover that his father, continuing to appeal for him, had contacted a friend of Philip Carteret who had forwarded such a good report on the lad, he'd decided to put him on the quarterdeck as Midshipman.

Much to Carteret's annoyance, though, Midshipman Newton didn't measure up to the good character he'd been portrayed as having. He soon reverted to being the idle, sullen wretch he'd been while in the merchant fleet. He was resentful of authority and discipline and showed neither respect nor gratitude to his captain for his promotion.

Rather than have compassion for those left below decks, John used his authority to add to their misery, bullying and humiliating them. This behavior was quite contrary to his determination to prove he was better than they were. Eventually, there were only two men left on board who still liked him as he'd alienated a lot of the senior officers, too. In one instance, ensuring that the man heard him, he openly announced that he could do a better job than the Bosun's Mate was doing.

Of his two remaining friends, one was James Mitchell, the ship's clerk who had advised John of his duties as a Junior Royal Naval Officer. The other was young Midshipman Job Lewis. When they first met, he'd sensed that John came from a good Christian home like himself. He was well mannered, didn't drink and, unlike his time as an Ordinary Merchant Seaman, he never swore and always sang the age-old shanties in their original form rather than adding bawdy lyrics.

With his promotion to Midshipman, John was no longer confined to ship and, with other officers, he often went ashore in the longboat, then took another boat to see Polly at her boarding school in Chatham. There, he took on the characteristics of his father, strutting about, boasting of the prize money that would shortly be his when his ship captured an enemy vessel. Believing he was creating a good impression, he was actually embarrassing Polly, for, like Captain Newton's neighbors, her companions mocked and made faces at him behind his back. Polly felt so humiliated she begged him never to come to The Young Lady's Seminary again but instead to wait until holiday times and then visit her at home.

By then Polly, who was sixteen, realized that John was in love with her. Although he never actually spoke of it, he hinted that once his ship sailed he could be away for a long time. And he begged her not to get too friendly with other young men after she left school and started mixing in adult society.

As always he often overstayed his leave, and although it maddened Captain Carteret, it wasn't terribly important while in port. Weeks passed but still there were no sailing orders.

Mathematics had never been John's strongest subject, and since he had aspirations of promotion all the way up to ship's captain, he would need a knowledge of navigation. So, to make use of the time, he bought a copy of Barrow's "Euclid's Elements of Geometry," which he intended to study with the same intensity as he'd read Shaftsbury's "Characteristics."

At last, in May, the *HMS Harwich* prepared to sail. By then, John was thoroughly bored and longing for action. But instead of going into battle with the enemy, duty rested in escorting convoys up and down the Scottish coast or else across to Norway.

This would have added to the tedium but in James Mitchell he'd found a delightful companion. He was good-natured, intelligent, and possessed a wonderful sense of humor. On uneventful watches, while leaning over the rail, he and John spent hours discussing philosophy and life's many mysteries. Inevitably, one night the conversation turned to religion when John referred to his favorite book and what it meant to him. To his surprise, James told him he was a Freethinker himself. He knew the book well and John had put a wrong interpretation on it. Shaftsbury didn't think people *misunderstood* God. What he'd said was, *there is no God. Who, of any intellect, needed a God?* Religion was nothing but a burden. Relinquish it and one gained freedom.

Though horrified, John demanded to know more. Happy to oblige, James expounded his theory. *God* was simply a means of ensuring people followed a certain code of behavior under the threat of being cast into hell on some mythical Day of Judgment. The promise of immortality in heaven was nothing more than bait. You only live once so make the most of it.

This was a tempting proposition and, in his mind, John began questioning the whole concept of a Deity—any Deity. To live without a conscience would be freedom indeed. He recalled the terror he had of his father over his own wanton disobedience. This he equated with sin and the subsequent wrath of God. If there was no God, no sin, no Day of Judgment and everlasting punishment, that would give total freedom of mind, body, and soul.

By midsummer, these ideas were so deeply instilled in his mind, he'd completely rejected all notion of God, sin, and everlasting life. The Prince of Glory was thrown overboard with the same disdain he'd tossed the ring in his nightmare. And, in a Norwegian fiord, there was no volcano to erupt into flame; nor did a stranger appear to retrieve his discarded faith from the icy waters and hold it in safekeeping for him.

Now, under Mitchell's influence, he couldn't wait to try out his new philosophy and the most likely candidate for corruption was the unsuspecting Job Lewis. John accused him of being a hypocrite for having religious beliefs. At every opportunity, he mocked his good, moral lifestyle, general courtesy, and obedient acceptance of rules and regulations.

Upset at this change in one he'd admired so much, Job vehemently defended his Christian faith and everything else he believed right and proper. Instead of the pleasant hours they'd once shared in intelligent discussions, raging arguments developed at almost every meeting.

6

The Deserter

One afternoon, heading down the east coast from Scotland after delivering a convoy, the lookout spotted three unidentified sails on the horizon. Allowing a period of twenty minutes in which the ships failed to show their colors, all hands were called on deck.

Orders were given to "Clear decks for action. Stand to the guns."

At full sail, the *HMS Harwich* gave chase for the next two hours, during which time two of the other ships broke away and sailed in opposite directions. At six o'clock, as the British ship was closing in, the remaining ship finally broke colors to reveal herself as the French Privateer, *Solide*.

The *Harwich* opened fire and the French retaliated, but missed. Over the next half hour, as the vessels drew closer, they continued firing. One broadside shot severely damaged the *Solide*. Still it kept firing. The *Harwich* was about to fire a second broadside when the enemy ship suddenly struck colors. To the cheers of Captain Carteret's men, a boarding party was quickly organized and the French captain was brought across to the *HMS*

Harwich, where he handed over his sword in an official act of surrender.

Both crews had come close to death but it had no effect on John Newton. The prize they'd captured would be sold to the Admiralty for conversion to a British Royal Naval vessel—an economic way of adding to the fleet without enormous building costs. The proceeds of the sale would be shared by all officers and crew and John could only think of what he would buy for Polly and how proud she would be of him.

Back on routine patrol, he relieved his boredom by studying geometry and by continuing to destroy Job Lewis's faith in himself and in God. Observing him closely, he began to notice a gradual change in the boy. He'd become withdrawn and went about with a permanent frown replacing his once happy grin.

In his heart, John started feeling some regret over what he was doing to him, while, at the same time, he convinced himself he was right. "But suppose you're not," whispered a small voice deep inside him.

His mother's goodness and teachings, together with those of David Jennings and Isaac Watts had put down roots that weren't easily discarded. If there was no afterlife, he would never see his dear mother again—but if there was no afterlife then he needn't fear a Day of Judgment either. In the dead of night, alone on watch, he was secretly afraid. In his hammock, sleep evaded him and he kept remembering the ring.

Still, by day, he was as boastful as ever about his freedom from morality.

In the winter of 1744, the *HMS Harwich* was anchored off Deal, Kent, and as Christmas approached John looked forward to the annual festivities at the Catletts. He so wanted to see Polly again, particularly as his ship was preparing to do a year's tour of duty in the Mediterranean. Then, days before going ashore, all leave was canceled when new orders arrived. Instead of going to the Mediterranean, they were joining a squadron of ships on a five-year voyage to the East Indies and the Cape of Good Hope.

This made little difference to the impressed men below decks but it wrecked all John's plans. On his return, he would be twenty-four and Polly, twenty. She could be married to someone else by then.

Days passed by, and still they were in Deal riding on single anchor, ready to sail as soon as a favorable wind blew up. The waiting devastated John until he was driven to ask for leave to go and say goodbye to Polly and ask her to wait for him.

The compassionate Philip Carteret granted him twenty-four hours, not knowing it would take all that time to ride the forty miles to Chatham and back again. Even by spending only minutes with Polly, if the weather turned against John, he couldn't make it back in the given time, but he didn't tell his captain that. On reaching shore, he quickly hired a livery horse and set off at full speed along the Canterbury Road.

Assuming he was there for Christmas, George and Elizabeth Catlett welcomed him with open arms and the children demanded to know all about his recent adventures. Eager as ever, he fell in with the festivities. If he was now steeped in atheism, he took great care to hide it from Polly and her family. No one would have suspected the hypocrisy that lay behind his carol-singing and churchgoing.

It was nearly a week later, by some chance remark, that they discovered he'd only been entitled to *one day's* leave. George was furious at his deception. And, being a Customs and Excise Officer, he was also bitterly angry and disappointed at John's irresponsible attitude toward his duty, especially in wartime, and he was ordered from the house.

By now it was obvious to everybody that he loved Polly, so her father forbade them to ever see or even write to each other again. When Elizabeth saw her daughter in tears, she wasn't quite so harsh and gave permission for them to write via Polly's aunt. She was visiting them at the time and lived a short distance away.

When John rejoined his ship on New Year's Day, the usually mild Captain Carteret raged at his insubordination. Yet, again, he was let off because overstaying leave wasn't as serious an offense as desertion.

John wrote often to Polly and got the QuarterMaster to put his letters on the mail coach to Kent during his visits ashore for provisions. Fearing the letters might fall into her father's hands, he didn't sign his name but used the monogram J superimposed onto the N—which would have fooled nobody.

Alas, because Polly was self-conscious about her terrible handwriting and her poor spelling, she never wrote back.

For four more weeks they were moored at Deal with John confined to ship. By the end of January he was almost demented, and in his last letter he finally found courage to tell her of his love. He said he was worried sick lest she forget him and asked her to wait for him, promising her vast riches from prize money on his return.

It wasn't until a blustery morning in February that they set sail. As they passed through the Strait of Dover and into the English Channel, John finally realized he was leaving Britain behind for five years, and considering the many hazards faced by mariners, maybe for good. On the *Harwich* sailed—only to drop anchor again at Spithead, a narrow stretch of water between the mainland and the Isle of Wight. With frustration mounting in the men, they stayed there for a further three weeks, waiting for the flagship *HMS Sutherland* to join them.

At last, the full squadron was gathered and it was a magnificent sight as, with billowing sails and pennants flying, the ships formed a convoy for a large fleet of East Indiamen and Guineamen. John looked enviously at the Guineamen, destined for a year's voyage to Africa while the East Indiamen would be absent for five years.

The fleet was three days out in the Atlantic when the winds suddenly changed and all ships were ordered back to take refuge in Torbay, Devon. No sooner had they dropped anchor when the winds changed again and orders went up to resume sailing. Unfortunately, a gross misjudgment had been made. As the fleet rounded Start Point, Cornwall, several of the ships, both merchant and Royal Naval, floundered and ran aground.

With the remaining ships, Commodore George Pocock, commander of the *HMS Sutherland*, carried on, leaving orders for the rest to follow when reloaded. It was days before they were ready, and Midshipman Newton was becoming increasingly unsettled at still being tied to England's shores while also being confined to ship.

Finally, on the last day of February, all was ready and, once more, the now diminished squadron set off in pursuit of the convoy. They were soon united but as the fleet rounded Lizard Point it was hit by a violent storm. All the vessels were blown off course, taking them close to treacherous rocks and putting them in danger of collision.

Throughout the rest of that day and moonless night, amid noise and confusion, men fought desperately to control their ships. More than once in those dark hours, the *HMS Harwich* came within feet of neighboring vessels. Philip Carteret prayed for God's help, but by morning most on board believed it was only the captain's superb seamanship that had saved her.

Dawn revealed a sad display of damage all around. Even the flagship had lost her mainmast and bowsprit, and the entire squadron was forced to limp into Plymouth, Devon, for repairs.

Work went on all through March and the men grew dispirited at the long delays. Anchored in Plymouth Sound, it was but a short swim to shore for a good swimmer. Almost every night, under cover of darkness, not only sailors but officers were slipping over the side.

By sheer chance, the Royal Africa Company had chosen Captain Newton as their representative to go to Dartmouth and collect a report on the damaged merchant ships. When John knew he was in

Devon, he begged his captain's permission to go and
see him. If he could talk to his father, he may be
able to persuade Carteret to transfer him to a Guineaman in exchange for a reliable merchant seaman. That way he would only be away for a year.
But eleven of his company had deserted already
and, with John's reputation, Captain Carteret
couldn't afford the risk,

However, a month later, when a longboat party
was going to collect fresh water, biscuits, and salt
meat, with few officers left to choose from, he asked
John to escort them to ensure no one deserted. Perhaps because Midshipman Newton had made no attempt to go over the side, he felt he could at last be
trusted.

He didn't know it wasn't duty that had kept him
from deserting; it was because John couldn't swim.
No sooner was the longboat moored when he leaped
from it, disappeared into the crowd on the quayside, and began the twenty-five-mile walk to see his
father. Meanwhile, unknown to him, his father was
busily arranging with an old colleague, Admiral
Nadeley, for his son's release into the Merchant
Navy.

All day John walked and at night, to escape de-
tection, he slept under a hedge in a field. Dawn saw
him on his way again; then, with less than a mile
to go and just as he'd spotted Dartmouth in the distance, he, too, was spotted by a marine patrol.
There was no mistaking the jaunty roll of a sailor.
And, for such a smartly dressed man—there were
no naval uniforms then—his lack of hand luggage
betrayed him instantly as a likely deserter.

John knew it was useless denying he was a

sailor so he lied that he was on leave—but he had
no documents to prove it. He was arrested and, with
several other captives, marched the twenty-five
miles back to Plymouth where they were locked up
in the town prison. The penalty for desertion from
the Royal Navy, especially in wartime, was hanging
from the yardarm or, if lucky, one hundred lashes.
Officers, on the other hand, were dealt with more
leniently. They could be court-martialled, but invariably their captain reduced the crime to being
absent without leave and they were privately caned
for their punishment.

Two days later, John was taken from prison and
rowed out to the *HMS Harwich*, which Admiral Nadeley, with his appeal for John's release, had
boarded only an hour earlier. But to no avail. Captain Carteret was adamant—this time, Midshipman Newton must be severely punished.

Clamped hand and foot in irons, John was put
below decks until the *HMS Harwich* had been at
sea for two days. Only then was he brought before
his captain to answer the charge of desertion.

On hearing the sentence, he was struck speech-
less. Not only would he be stripped of officer rank,
but before the entire ship's company he would be
physically stripped and severely flogged until
senseless.

No longer the swaggering braggart, helpless in
the strong grip of former comrades, he was uncer-
emoniously dragged up on deck where he was
spread-eagled and tied to a frame. An added insult
was seeing the man administering the punishment
was none other than the Bosun's Mate whom he'd
so often maligned and ridiculed.

While some gloated, most of the officers called

to witness the punishment felt pity at seeing one of their own in so degrading a situation. James Mitchell and young Job Lewis were among them.

John steeled himself against the pain about to be inflicted on his bare flesh. But when the first drum-roll ended and the cat o' nine tails descended, it was as if the very flames from the volcano he'd seen when he threw away the ring had entered his body. Soon he was unable to count and the drum-rolls had merged into one prolonged sound. But on and on the punishment continued until he was, indeed, senseless.

Although one hundred lashes was the correct number for his crime, after twenty-four, the semi-conscious man was untied and taken belowdecks for medical examination. On Captain Carteret's ship no kelt was rubbed into open wounds to either add to the agony or to facilitate healing.

When John came around, the surgeon passed him fit for duty and he was ordered back on deck. Racked with pain, he dragged his lacerated body along. Having forfeited the power to abuse and debase men of lesser ranks, he was now the recipient of their scorn. Even Job refused to acknowledge him at all. Mitchell still sympathized with him, though, and tried to protect him from the taunts and verbal attacks, but arrogant as ever, John rejected his friendship and now he hadn't a friend on board.

Slowly, his back began to heal but his pride didn't. He refused to believe he deserved so drastic a punishment and felt like murdering the captain. He couldn't concentrate on anything for he spent this time thinking up various means of getting rid of him. He even contemplated suicide.

7

Into the Slave Trade

When the fleet reached Madeira in May, the *HMS Harwich* needed some repairs so she was taken into shallow water. When they were done, John was among the men set to painting her with hot tar. The last time was in freezing, windy weather, but on this occasion the sun beat down on his raw back till it was a mass of blisters. Like a mad dog, he growled and snarled at everyone who came near him.

It took a week to complete that task. The next job was loading provisions for the second stage of the voyage to the Cape of Good Hope, the southernmost tip of Africa, before crossing the Indian Ocean and on to the East Indies. Trading with India and China, the East Indiamen carried luxurious cargoes of silks, porcelain, spices, opium, perfumes and tea—a costly commodity in the eighteenth century. The ships were the elite of the ocean and their captains the wealthiest. Yet, along with their crews, they were also the most endangered of merchant mariners.

With such riches aboard they were prey for marauding privateers so, unlike most merchant vessels, the huge ships were as heavily armed as any warship. And, when moving in large convoys, they needed the added security of a Royal Naval escort.

On such a run, months went by without the convoy touching land. Their diet consisted of salted pork and beef, dried fish, cheese, butter, ground peas and hardtack. There were no vegetables or fruit. As water soon became stagnant and undrinkable, they were allowed eight pints of ale a day which was usually bad.

Unscrupulous victualers regularly sold rancid food and stale ale that, within one week at sea, was rotten and fit only to go over the side. Hardtack was the only food they could rely on but even that got full of fat, black maggots. To dislodge them, the men rapped the biscuits on the edge of the table, but in the dim light below deck there was no guarantee they'd succeeded. The more sensitive among them shut their eyes to avoid seeing what they were biting into. All kinds of strange diseases, fevers, scurvy, and cholera raged.

Ships' navigators faced the confusion of inaccurate charts and compass deviation when any iron on board could cause the needle to vary as much as six degrees, thus throwing a ship right off course.

John contemplated on all of this while he lifted heavy sacks, crates, and barrels onto his scarred shoulders and back—now scorched under the fiery sun. For a fleeting moment his mind went back over the years to his cozy London home and his mother's tenderness. Even his father's sternness was a pleasant memory. So much had gone wrong in the few years from leaving childhood behind. If he'd gone into the church . . . but he'd grown too wise for that sort of nonsense.

"God!" As he spat the offending word from his lips, pain swept over him when a cane thwacked across his raw shoulders jolting him back to the present. Nostalgia quickly vanished and he returned to the unhappy existence he'd brought upon himself.

That night, lying face down, he slept like the dead and didn't hear the Bosun's whistle at dawn. Nobody cared if John got into trouble or not, so they didn't bother to wake him. When Job Lewis came belowdecks to make his daily check, he found his old friend still asleep and compassion overwhelmed him. With a friendly comment, he gently prodded him and John awoke with a start. But instead of leaping from the hammock, he deliberately provoked his former friend by yawning, stretching, and generally dawdling.

This made Job so angry, he took his knife from his belt and slashed the hammock rope. With a thud, John fell to the deck and rolled over on to his painful back. Subdued, he quickly dressed, packed away his hammock and went on deck to continue loading provisions in readiness for sailing the next day.

When a small boat pulled alongside he was only slightly curious until one of the *Harwich* men, with his sailor's bed-roll tucked under his arm, came on deck and walked to the ship's rail. He threw the bundle into the boat then heaved his legs over the rail and began scrambling down the ladder.

"Where's he going? What's going on?" John asked, and was told. Captain Carteret had exercised his right and pressed two chippies—carpenters—from a Guineaman moored nearby, In turn, the merchant captain asked for two ordinary seamen to take their place but had been granted only one.

John started running round in a frenzy, asking the officer in charge of the boat to wait while he found the lieutenant to get him to ask Captain Carteret to let him go too. The lieutenant laughed at his chances but asked all the same. To his amazement, the captain gave his permission. He didn't fancy another five years of John Newton on his ship.

In less than an hour after being ejected from his hammock, John had left the Royal Navy and was heading for a fresh start. The ship was bound for West Africa with a cargo of cutlery, wool, and guns in exchange for gold and ivory, but mostly slaves. A "separate trader," she had no ties with the Royal Africa Company but was obliged to pay them a percentage of her profit from the slave trade.

No one on board, not even the man who had gone with him, knew John was once a Christian. That left him free to live as he wanted, uncluttered by morals and decency. The conscience-stabbing presence of Job Lewis was also behind him. What's more, he would be back in England within the year.

It turned out, however, that the merchant captain had known John's father and was under the impression he'd gained a good man. Welcoming his son aboard, he signed him on as foremastman—the rank directly below petty-officer. Like Carteret, he was soon disillusioned though, for almost immediately John started making a nuisance of himself.

He was lazy, disobedient, and foul-mouthed. At Sunday service he noted the few who took their devotions seriously, then mocked them and set about destroying their faith. He was always finding fault with the captain's orders and criticized his seamanship. He made up obscene songs about him, about the First Mate, and all the officers. Then he taught them to the rest of the crew. On what had been a happy ship, within days he tried to rouse the men to mutiny.

There was one man on board, however, whom John admired, Mr. Clow. After fighting his way up from dire poverty he was now a very rich man and part-owner of the vessel they were sailing on.

Known as a Resident Trader, he bought slaves from African slavers and kept them in his fortress until he resold them at a profit. These *fortresses* situated along the Grain Coast—now Sierra Leone— were armed complexes where white traders in ivory, gold, gems, and slaves, lived and ruled with a trained army of Africans.

Clow wasn't settled there though because the land was only good for growing coconuts and rice. He was moving to one of the three Plantain Islands to plant lime groves. He would build a new factory with living quarters for the slaves and a big house for himself and his wife, Pey Ey, an African princess.

For six months the ship would trade up and down, gradually filling the holds with living cargo. Then, when they reached a stretch of the coast near Clow's island, he was going to leave the ship while she set sail on the long haul from Africa to the West Indies—the Middle Passage, as it was called—

where the slaves would be sold. A fresh cargo of sugar, rum, and spices would then be taken on board and the ship would head back to England. There she would discharge her cargo, take on a fresh one, and head back for Africa. This was known as the Triangular Trade.

Chained together in groups of fifteen, slaves were brought aboard and branded with hot irons before being herded into the holds. Being a Separate Trader, this ship carried other cargo as well, so the conditions belowdecks weren't quite as bad as on other ships kept solely for slaving. Nevertheless, there was always a lot of sickness and fevers among both slaves and crew. If some officers and men were sick and others were ashore bartering, there could be as few as twelve men supervising 200 hostile slaves. To avoid trouble, they were brought up on deck tied in pairs and tethered to well-separated iron rings set in the decks for a short spell each day. The rest of the time they were kept locked in the holds.

In exchange for the goods white traders had to offer, the majority of slaves were sold by African chiefs or kings. They had usually been taken prisoner in tribal conflicts and were brought from as far as one thousand miles away; all were from different tribes and, often, spoke different languages. Occasionally, though, when there was a scarcity, ships' crews would sneak ashore at night, advance on sleeping villages and abduct men, women, and children.

This mission was going particularly well until, just as it was nearing completion, on New Year's Day 1746, while at anchor at the mouth of the Sherbro River, the captain suddenly took ill and died within hours.

In the absence of a captain, the First Mate always takes over and, of course, in this instance he was one of the men John had composed an offensive song about. Now, bent on revenge, the new captain threatened to hand him back to the first Royal Navy ship they met.

John could think of no worse fate. With his friend Clow sharing ownership of the vessel and the First Mate merely deputizing for a captain, he could have had trouble trying to carry out his threat. But Mr. Clow was leaving the ship the next day and there would be no one left to defend him, so John persuaded him to take him with him.

Clow was always amused by John's high spirits and had grown quite fond of the intelligent, darkly handsome young man with the soulful eyes. He was delighted to take him into his employ with a view to making him his business partner someday. All they needed was John's release from the ship, and, as the acting captain was eager to be rid of him, it was granted.

Next morning, he quickly gathered his few pathetic belongings, together with his two treasured books, and stuffed them into his bundle. With six months' wages jingling in his pocket John left the ship and set off for Clow's new island home, one hundred miles to the south.

Two of the three Plantain Islands were covered with coconut palms and banana trees, but the third, Mr. Clow's, had only rice and a dense forest crawling with snakes. However, although a mere two miles in circumference, it was the biggest island and it had a lot of potential.

Straightaway, Clow set about getting his compound under way, consisting of a warehouse, living-quarters for slaves, a large house for himself, and a series of smaller houses, including one for John. All the buildings were of coconut logs roofed with banana leaf thatch. He was also given a patch of ground for keeping hens, and the slaves planted vegetables for him. Clow gave him some odd bits of furniture and he was soon settled into his new home.

Next began the cultivation of the land with slaves planting pineapples and paw-paws. The lime grove was going to be a bigger project, so it was left until later in the year.

When all was completed, Clow left in his shallop—a light, two-masted craft with a cabin below-decks—to go and bring Pey Ey from her native island many hundreds of miles away.

The work had taken many months, by which time Mr. Clow had made John his partner and always left him in charge of everything in his absence. Almost 21, John was happier than he'd been in years. At last he had power over people and was treated like a king—something that had been promised to him when he was headed for Jamaica. Even so, sometimes, at the end of the day, he thought wistfully of Polly and wondered if they would ever meet again.

Alas, John's newfound happiness lasted only a short time, for when Clow returned with his young wife she took an instant dislike to him. In her own tribe, Pey Ey was a princess and she had the beauty and bearing befitting her rank. She always wore rows and rows of gold necklaces and huge golden hoop earrings. Her bracelets and rings were shaped like tiny sets of cymbals that jingled when she moved. And in each hand she carried dainty silver bells that tinkled as she walked.

Besides her physical beauty, Pey Ey was a charming woman who had taken the trouble to learn some of the white man's culture and etiquette. She presided over a well-run household and kept a table fit for any king.

Clow was fully aware that it was due to his wife's lofty position in African society that he had prospered so well in all his trading with kings, tribal chiefs, and village elders, and he adored her. Nevertheless, she resented John's involvement in the business and his sharing the profits. She was envious of the two Englishmen spending a lot of time together, and she felt inferior when she heard her husband conversing with the educated young man on all sorts of intellectual topics she knew nothing about. When he informed her that he looked upon John as a son, it inflamed her jealousy all the more and she was livid with rage.

Despite being of high birth, Pey Ey knew she would always be at a disadvantage with any white person. She and Clow had married within the laws of her tribe, but the union would never be recognized outside that community. If he ever decided to retire and return to Europe, what would become of her, she wondered? In the eighteenth century no society outside of Africa would accept a white person with a black spouse. Although of high-ranking parentage, her husband could tire of her and abandon her, ousting her of her position as mistress of all he possessed in favor of his *adopted* son.

Shortly after she arrived on the island, her husband and John were due to sail on a two-month trading expedition, but before they could leave John took ill with a fever. For days he rambled incoherently as his temperature soared to a dangerous level. Few white men survived if they caught those fevers before they were properly acclimatized and Clow was very concerned. He couldn't delay his departure, yet he wondered if he would see his young friend alive again. The best he could do was leave instructions for him to be well cared for. He also gave orders for the estate to be managed the way John had run it when he was left behind while Clow went to collect Pey Ey.

As soon as he had sailed, Pey Ey took the opportunity to vent her hatred on John. She ordered him to be carried from his house and taken to the warehouse where he was placed on a wooden case with a log of wood for a pillow. She then proclaimed herself Queen of the island and took over the management of the estate and the business.

8

Enslaved

For most of his illness, John was semi-conscious, so he knew little of what was happening. Pey Ey often visited the warehouse and stood looking down at him while he raved in his delirium and begged for water, which she refused to give him. Sometimes, when the overseers weren't around, the slaves managed to give him a few drops of their own allowance.

Gradually, the fever started to subside and, as his temperature dropped, John became aware of what was happening. Only then did he begin to *feel* ill, but the slaves working nearby convinced him he had been far worse and was now actually getting better. Still, he couldn't raise his head from his wooden pillow.

When Pey Ey saw he was recovering she was clearly disappointed. He was starting to feel hunger again, so she refused him food as well as water. On one of her visits she stood smiling down at John, then turned and went into the main house for her evening meal. Later a servant came out bearing a plate, which he gave to the sick man. On it were the remains of Pey Ey's dinner; some bones, skin, and gristle—and being so hungry he ate them ravenously.

Next evening at dinnertime he was ordered to go to the house. He could barely stand but was afraid to disobey, so he slowly struggled to his feet. Hanging on to fences he staggered along. On reaching the house he was taken into the dining room where Pey Ey sat at the head of the table. It was laden with plates and bowls of sumptuous chicken, fish, rice, fruit, and goblets of wine. For a moment John thought she'd relented, or perhaps she was afraid of Clow returning and discovering how he'd been ill-treated.

Although she could see he was rocking on his feet he was kept standing. Then she handed him a plate. Once more, it was her scraps; a few grains of rice and a fish's skeleton. He took it eagerly but being so weak, he dropped it, the plate smashing to pieces as it landed on the floor. Pey Ey threw back her head and laughed her cruel laugh, then demanded he be taken from her sight.

That night, with hunger pains clutching at his insides, he waited until everything was quiet, then, on all fours, he crawled from the building and went around the back into the field. There he clawed at the earth with his bony hands until he managed to dig up some roots, which he devoured. They were so revolting, no sooner had he swallowed them than he vomited them up again and crawled back to the warehouse. As inedible as his meal had been, he returned to the field the following night and the night after. Each time he ate the dreadful roots he was sick, but at least it kept the hunger pangs away.

How he longed for Clow's return, but that

wouldn't be for a long time and he doubted he would still be alive then. Somehow the slaves found out what he was doing and, chained together in pairs, they started sneaking out of their quarters in the dead of night to smuggle him a small portion of their own meager rice rations. John felt they were ashamed that Pey Ey, one of their own people, should treat him so badly. Oddly enough, this made no impression on his attitude toward slavery which, even when a child and a devout Christian, he'd thought was right and proper.

Since Clow had made the island habitable, people from the mainland settled there and established villages—or *kraals*—of wattle and daub houses. On hearing that the Queen of the island owned a *white* slave they were filled with curiosity. Under cover of darkness they paid secret visits to Clow's fortress to view this phenomenon and take him food as one would an animal in a zoo. These morsels, together with the bits the slaves fed him, sustained him during what should, under other circumstances, have been his convalescent period.

By some miracle, Newton survived the illness, the dehydration, starvation, and general maltreatment. That made Pey Ey so furious she resorted to another form of persecution. While he was still hardly able to stand and could only drag his feet, she forced him to walk around her room while her slaves were ordered to trail behind, limping and mocking. This sent Pey Ey into hysterical laughter. She clapped her hands for joy, then threw rotten fruit, vegetables, and even stones at him and ordered her servants to follow suit. They all sympathized with John but knew if they disobeyed their fate would be worse than his.

When he heard Clow had returned, John believed he would soon be rescued like the time he was press-ganged and his father came. But Pey Ey told her husband a string of lies about how badly John had behaved toward her and how he had mismanaged the business. When confronted with these accusations, John told him the truth but Clow believed his wife.

He was now ready to have the lime grove planted, and instead of sending John to oversee the slaves, Clow put him to work beside them in the fields as punishment. For hours he was stooped, planting row upon row of the tiny shoots under the blazing sun and the lash from an African overseer. Sadly, due to ignorance, in those days for a white man to find himself in an inferior position to a black man was the height of degradation and humiliation.

When it came time for Clow to embark on another mission, to safeguard his wife and property, he took John with him on the shallop.

Not being the most honest of men, Clow went trading on another man's territory from which he made a good profit. Seeing how well John conducted the business, he was just beginning to trust him again when the trader, whose land he'd exploited, came back to discover there were no slaves left for him to barter with. In a rage at how he'd been tricked, he determined to cause trouble between the two partners and told Clow that John had been stealing his goods and selling them while he was trading ashore. Recalling what his wife had told him, Clow believed it.

The next time he left his boat, he was going away for two days and nights and taking his servants with him. To ensure John didn't steal from him again in his absence, Clow had him tied up and tethered to the ship's rail with a padlock. Yet, before embarking on his trading mission, he was going to dine with the very man he himself had duped and who had told him such lies about John.

All John was left with was a small bowl of rice. He was wearing a thin cotton shirt, some tattered trousers and, on his head, a knotted handkerchief to keep him from the heat of the sun. On the second day it rained torrentially and his clothes steamed on his body. Although still warm, compared to the heat of the day, once the temperature dropped at night there was a distinct chill in the air. This was particularly noticeable to someone in his undernourished state, clad in saturated clothing, and weak from his recent illness. Shivering uncontrollably he sometimes hallucinated and lost all sense of reality.

On Clow's return John soon detected the smell of cooking fowl, but his share consisted of some uncooked chicken innards which quickly turned rotten in the heat. Hungry though he was, the very thought of eating the putrid offal made him retch. Instead he used it as bait and, trailing it in the water, he managed to catch a fish which he had to eat raw. Nevertheless, with Clow back on board, John was freed from the ship's rail and allowed to sleep below deck with the servants.

The next night he fared slightly better with the

food. Following the smell of cooking fowl emitting from the cabin, he was presented with a *fresh* uncooked chicken wing. But it was still covered with feathers, so that too served as fish bait.

It was the same pattern each time Clow went ashore. One night there was a tornado—a sudden, whirling wind that threatened to destroy everything in its path. The boat spun on its moorings and was tossed right out of the water. John, bound and helpless on deck, was pitched in all directions.

At the end of three months they returned to the island where he expected to be set to work again on the plantation alongside Clow's slaves. This time, though, further torment was to be inflicted upon him. Before planting the very limes by which he and Clow had intended to make another fortune, John was taken to the forge where the smith clamped him in heavy, flesh-cutting ankle-irons to eliminate any possibility of escape.

Clow and Pey Ey made a habit of coming to watch and make cruel jibes as he worked. "You may escape from here, one day, and return to England. You may even get command of your own ship and come back and buy these fruits you are planting," scoffed Clow, accompanied by peals of laughter from his wife.

Much as they resented white men, all the slaves felt compassion for John at his treatment from one of his own kind just as they'd felt shame at Pey Ey's behavior toward him. Servants secretly brought food from the house together with paper, quills, and ink that he'd asked for.

John had a theory that if a letter to his father could be taken onto one of the ships putting in at the island on its way back to Britain—or anywhere in Europe—he stood a chance of being rescued. The problem was, how to get such a letter on board?

Embarrassed at his plight, fettered, sun-blistered, and almost skeletal in appearance, he hid from anyone coming ashore. Clow was a respected man and any story he concocted about John's misdeeds and subsequent punishment would be accepted; particularly by anyone who happened to know of John's reputation. His only opportunity was to persuade one of the house servants to smuggle his letter on board by slipping it into Clow's mailbag. Using this method, over the next weeks he wrote three letters to Captain Newton telling him of his situation and his despair. Would he, please, help him—but only on condition that he was forgiven for all his misdeeds.

John knew it could take months, or well over a year, for the letters to reach England, especially if a ship was bound for the middle-passage. Still, he lived in hope. He often worried about losing his sanity and devised a way to keep his brain active. On nights when the moon was bright, despite being hampered by his shackles, he would steal away to the lime grove. And, squatting on the ground with his geometry book, he drew diagrams in the dirt with a stick. At other times he chose a small cove where he used the damp sand as a drawing board.

When another English trader moved on to the island he went to acquaint himself with Clow. Being the better businessman of the two, proof of his affluence lay in the fact he had a host of *white servants* rather than *black slaves*. Therefore, he was amazed to see a white man actually slaving for another white man. Still, Clow assured him that John wasn't a slave at all but a servant serving a term of punishment for some misdemeanor.

The newcomer, however, wasn't as convinced as he appeared to be because, although he spent a lot of time away from his home, whenever he returned he always noticed that John's *punishment* continued.

One night, while sailing close in shore, heading back to his end of the island, he spotted the young man hobbling along the sand only to disappear into a small opening in the rocks. The following morning the trader went to investigate and discovered the complicated geometrical drawings in the sand. This aroused his suspicions even more about Clow's story and he made an excuse to visit him.

Pey Ey sensed the man was prying and warned her husband. If it became widely known they had a *white* slave, there could be trouble from other traders. Mindful of this and fearful that John may soon die from his maltreatment anyway, Clow suggested the other man take him in his employ as "he couldn't control him."

Thus, in November 1746, John was given the release he'd longed for but never really hoped to gain.

The man took him across to his home where he was given soap and water to bathe with, a luxury he'd almost forgotten. Afterwards he was given clean clothes and the first proper meal in a year. Of course the whole story came out and the trader, determined to make up for all John had suffered, put him in charge of his household. Whenever he left on an expedition, just as Clow had once done, he left John to deal with the business and the accounts, entrusting him with thousands of pounds.

Feeling he'd been restored to his proper position in the world and thankful for it, John worked diligently for his new employer who, on his return, found everything in perfect order. This worried the man, though, for Clow and Pey Ey couldn't afford to let it be known that the man they'd accused of all sorts of crimes and misdeeds had suddenly proved himself trustworthy. Thus John's employer determined to get him away from the island as soon as possible lest anything happen to him.

He'd just built a new factory and his young English manager was having difficulty running it single-handedly. He needed an assistant desperately, so his employer invited him to a meeting where he introduced him to John. They felt sure they could work together, so they were sent off to build up the company at Kittam, one hundred miles away.

9

"Gone Black"

*B*oth men became firm friends and business
prospered. Working as a team, while one
stayed behind overseeing the compound and
the planting of pumpkins and watermelon, the
other went off up-country, buying slaves in return
for goods. After a while, John proved to be the best
one at conducting that side of the business, so he
took on the job permanently.

The rivers of Sierra Leone have many small
tributaries which, in turn, have their own inlets
running hundreds of miles inland. Along these waterways John sailed, often navigating crocodile-infested stretches where huge snakes swam close by
his boat. Another hazard was hippopotami. Though
usually content to bask in the mud close by the riverbank, they would sometimes rise up as the boat
was passing, causing it to nearly capsize.

John stopped at all the villages along the river
to buy or barter for their ivory, wood-carvings, gold,
precious or semi-precious stones, and slaves. Accompanied by a few porters, he then went on long
treks farther inland to do more bargaining.

Many traders duped the Africans by such devious methods as diluting alcohol with water and putting false tops on barrels to make them appear bigger and thus holding more. They also unfolded bolts of cloth, cut huge chunks from the middle, then rolled them up again. These, along with other tricks, were commonplace but, despite John's shortcomings, he was an honest man who dealt fairly with his clients.

Knowing this, the natives were very friendly toward him and he was made welcome at every village. Their homes, long open-sided huts without doors, windows or any other kind of security, were crammed with the treasures that lured—often unscrupulous—traders from halfway across the world. Yet John was so respected he slept in their homes, confident that none of his goods would be stolen in the night and knowing the villagers trusted him with theirs.

He would frequently be left there alone or with the women and children while the men went hunting in the jungle or fishing in their hollowed out, tree-trunk canoes. In the hunters' absence, old men cast nets into the water from the shore and children hauled in any fish they'd managed to catch. This helped feed the villagers left behind. They had a form of civilization that included laws, art, and music. As well as painting and carving, they made cloth, jewelry, and pottery. The women grew corn and rice, and the children played various traditional games.

At night, seated in a circle around a blazing fire, John's blood surged through his veins and his heart pounded at the sound of primitive drums beating out the rhythm for the increasingly frenzied dancers. Extremely superstitious people, they were more in awe of the witch doctor than their tribal chief. They worshiped all sorts of gods, totems, and talismans and saw evil spirits in the most innocuous happenings, artifacts, or even in dead plants.

Because of all this superstition, coupled with ignorance, the natives indulged in some barbaric practices to which, although at first horrified, John gradually grew accustomed. In the short space of time that he'd been in Africa, he had "gone black," a term used for white men who had become inured to the atrocities.

He witnessed animal sacrifice—a token of thanks for a good harvest. There was human sacrifice too, some involving newborn babies, for twins were considered bad luck as one was believed to be an evil spirit. But since no one could tell which one was evil, they were both put to death at birth and their mother driven from the village for bringing a curse upon it.

If a chief's slave died and left very young children, they were either murdered or simply left to die since no one could be bothered rearing them. Older ones were spared to become slaves themselves. On the death of a chief his wives and slaves were also put to death.

They seriously believed that men from the Bulon tribe were able to turn themselves into leopards. If a wild animal attacked anyone or carried off a child, they accused the Bulons of having done it in the guise of leopards. This frequently resulted in tribal warfare and any prisoners taken were sold off as slaves—sometimes to John Newton.

Cannibalism, however, was largely a myth that

had gained its widespread notoriety through tribes accusing their enemies of it, as it was the most heinous crime one could commit. Those who partook of human flesh were a few feared tribal chiefs who were considered insane; and none of them lived within hundreds of miles of Sierra Leone. Ironically, the Africans thought cannibalism was the white man's practice, and when captured they believed they were being shipped away to be butchered and eaten.

Therefore, despite the lurid tales of cannibalistic savages recounted by travelers, on John Newton's treks up country, the danger was all from snakes and wild beasts, mostly wild cats and hyenas rather than lions or elephants.

After some months of this life, John stopped hoping for rescue, for quite on the contrary, there was nothing to be rescued from. He enjoyed the adventurous trips to outlying settlements. Back at his home in the compound he lived in luxury, with servants. He took an African "wife" who also waited on him hand and foot, and he was experiencing the very life Joseph Manesty had promised he would live in Jamaica; living like a king.

He'd had no replies to the letters he'd secretly dispatched to his father via Clow's mailbag. Nor was there any guarantee they had actually been sent. It was possible they'd been discovered before leaving the island. John knew Clow wouldn't have let him know that, preferring instead to let him think they were on their way to England.

The truth was, all the letters had arrived. But even before that, Captain Newton had begun searching for John after learning that he'd left the

HMS Harwich to rejoin the Merchant fleet, which he'd then left to go and work for a planter. He contacted the captain of every ship heading for Sierra Leone, asking him to make enquiries wherever he went to seek out his son. The first of those ships had continued their voyages on the Middle-Passage and hadn't yet returned to England either with or without news.

The letters explaining John's plight, if not the precise location of Clow's island, had arrived just as his father learned that Joseph Manesty had extended his trade to West Africa. Once more, he approached him for help, though he doubted he would get it after John had so flagrantly scorned his Jamaican offer. But to his relief, Joseph offered to trace the prodigal. Furthermore, his ship, the *Greyhound*, was sailing that very week, so he instructed her captain to find John and bring him home.

On reaching Africa, the merchantman traded up and down the coast for five months, and at every call its captain enquired of a young man by the name of John Newton. Hardly anyone had heard of him and those who had didn't know where he was.

Eventually, the *Greyhound* arrived at the Benanoe Islands where someone knew all about the young trader and told the captain where to find Clow's island. He also told him John was no longer there. He'd left almost a year earlier to go and work hundreds of miles inland. At this, the captain relinquished all hope of finding him and of keeping the reward Captain Newton had promised him for his son's safe return.

Meanwhile, at Kittam, John was preparing to leave for one of his trips inland. However, when he and his partner surveyed their stock of merchandise, there wasn't enough to justify his setting out on the journey.

As ships didn't stop at Kittam, all their trading goods and provisions were delivered to them either overland or by small inshore boats—and the latest consignments were long overdue. Under these circumstances, islanders waited until a passing merchantman came into view. Then a fire on the beach was lit and a "smoke" created to signal that they wished to trade. This method was never used at Kittam, though, for big ships either passed in the night or steered too far from shore to see a smoke signal.

After waiting three more days without the arrival of the expected goods, on the fourth morning John decided to set off that afternoon with his meager supplies. By leaving at that hour, by the time he made camp in the evening, the party would be too far away from the village for the porters to sneak back to spend the night in their own homes. This would ensure they were all present when it was time to set off again at dawn.

While John prepared for the trip, his partner wandered down to the beach to take a last look along the coast for the expected supplies. To his astonishment, rather than a small inshore boat, he saw the great flapping sails of a Guineaman slipping by. Had he gone there only fifteen minutes later, it would have sailed beyond his reach. He ordered his men to quickly put up a "smoke" to attract the merchant's attention and hoped it wasn't already too late.

On board the *Greyhound*, the lookout was about

to turn his gaze toward the open sea when he saw the first faint wisp of smoke on shore. The ship dropped anchor and the crew watched as some canoes were rowed toward them.

After buying the necessary items and seeing the canoes loaded, the trader was climbing back into his own boat when the captain casually asked if he'd ever heard of a John Newton in those parts.

Thirty minutes later he was ashore. And, standing in the middle of a luxurious living room overlooking an open veranda, he was heartily shaking hands with the young man he'd abandoned all hope of ever finding.

John was delighted at hearing his father had been trying to trace him even before he'd been asked to. Of course, there was no point in asking the *Greyhound*'s captain about Polly for he wouldn't know of her existence. But despite his pleasure in being found, John was so contented with his life, he didn't want to leave. He had grown to love Africa. He liked his work. He was happy with his tribal wife. And he had his comfortable thatched wattle and daub house where servants obeyed his every command.

But, thinking of Captain Newton's promised reward for bringing his son home safely, the ship's captain was determined John should leave. Hastily he made up a story that an elderly relative had died and left him a legacy of £400 a year. John couldn't think of any elderly relatives and when he asked for proof, the captain said he'd forgotten to bring the relevant documents with him. Although suspicious, in 1747, £400 a year was a fortune, enough to persuade him to return to England.

As quickly as he'd left the Royal Navy for the Merchant fleet at Madeira and with the same speed from which he'd resigned that to become Clow's assistant, he resigned from his post, left his African wife well provided for and, within an hour, was being rowed out to board the *Greyhound*. He was to travel as *super-cargo*; an unpaying passenger who would share the captain's cabin, eat at the captain's table and, though an experienced naval officer, wouldn't be obliged to perform any shipboard duties.

The ship wasn't a slaver but a general trader in such commodities as beeswax, created by bees and used for making floor and furniture polish; camwood, a hard, red, light wood used for making dyes and violin bows; ivory, and also gold that the natives dragged up from riverbeds.

Whereas slavers' holds were filled within months of arriving in Africa, this type of cargo took more than a year to collect, so from Kittam, the *Greyhound* was sailing 1,000 miles south to complete her mission.

At the first opportunity, John wrote to his father telling him of how he'd been found and that he was on his way home.

Due to sickness and deaths among the crew its numbers were reduced from twenty to twelve, consequently the ship was seriously undermanned. Of the few remaining, none took kindly to John making up the number on board to an unlucky thirteen. Still, he was a passenger rather than *one of them*, so they tried to disregard his presence as an ill-omen. All the same, they would have been grateful for his assistance from time to time.

The captain, too, fully expected John to waive his rights and help out in some way. He could have taken over the accounts, leaving the captain to his naval duties, or else he could have taken on some of those duties himself. But like many others before him, the *Greyhound*'s captain soon discovered that the twenty-one-year-old John Newton was not the caliber of man he'd been led to expect. He was idle and insolent. And after almost two years of having to be courteous to people he was dependent upon, he couldn't wait to vent his frustration.

10

Changing Winds

Throughout the past months, John's only thoughts of God had been of the pagan kind. Now, his mind turned to Jesus—Isaac Watt's "Young Prince of Glory"—though not to worship or give thanks for his deliverance, but to find out who were the Christians on board so that he could set about destroying their faith. It turned out that the captain was the only one.

John reveled in the use of foul language, gross profanities, and blasphemies, especially when the captain was within earshot. Only recently, though John didn't know it, Parliament had passed the Profane Oaths Act, forbidding profanities. Of course, the law of God had been in effect long before the Parliament's Act, but it had never deterred John Newton. The captain could have had a crew member punished for the offense, but there was nothing he could do to stop a passenger. And anyway, he had to consider the reward he would claim for recovering that particular passenger, so he dare not risk antagonizing him.

John reveled so much in his power over the ship's master, he was driven to *inventing* oaths, which were gleefully seized upon by his own kind on board.

Not being a slaver, when the holds were fully laden, the *Greyhound* made straight for home rather than the Middle-Passage but it was on an almost identical route. Having a lightweight cargo, rather than the heavy-laden slave ships with their human freight, the *Greyhound* rode high on the waterline. In the mildest breeze she could get up speeds that, on any other ship, would take up most of the sails. Such buoyancy also provided greater safety in adverse weather conditions.

The first call after leaving the west coast of Africa was at Annabonda Island, 300 miles out in the Atlantic. There they stocked up with cases of grain and kegs of fresh water, pigs and sheep to be killed and eaten on the long voyage, together with poultry and goats which would provide eggs and milk before they too were slaughtered for their meat. These necessary provisions actually weighed more than the cargo, but the captain hoped it would sustain them for the entire voyage without having to put in anywhere else en route. As the voyage continued and the stores were consumed, the weight would naturally depreciate anyway before they ran into known storm areas.

At last, they broke anchor for the voyage home to England. Determined by currents, trade winds, and a desire to skirt the mid-Atlantic doldrums where vessels lay becalmed for weeks, the course set would take them on an incredible seven-thousand-mile route. The first stretch of this complicated voyage was right across the south Atlantic to Guyana on the north coast of South America. From there they would sail north until, two months out from Annabonda, they reached the Labrador Sea and the southern tip of Newfoundland. Steering an eastern path to almost mid-Atlantic, they would then make a dog-leg turn north again to the southern tip of Greenland; east again to southern Iceland, and finally veer southeast for Britain.

It was January 1748, nine months since John Newton joined the ship and, by then, almost everyone on board hated him. Even the hardened ones were sickened by his uncouth conduct and foul language, and above all, by his profanities which were getting worse by the day. He made up disgusting stories based on the gospels; biblical names were corrupted, saints were mocked, and the words and teachings of Jesus ridiculed.

Finding the long voyage tedious, John, already *au fait* with every word in *Characteristics* and every diagram in Euclid's *Elements of Geometry*, decided to browse through some books he'd noticed lying on a shelf in the Captain's cabin. Ironically, they were all religious books.

At first he read them as works of fiction and found them entertaining and comical. Yet, at the same time, there was something about them that made him feel uncomfortable. One passage he found particularly disturbing: "So all sufficient, so delightful, so heavenly sweet is the friendship and company of Jesus."

For a moment he recalled the heavenly delight of having Jesus in his soul. He remembered how secure, how simple his life had been then, and he thought of the hundreds of thousands who shared— or believed they shared—the friendship and comfort of Jesus. How stupid they were! But *hundreds of thousands*, spread throughout the world—could so many be that stupid? His doubt was quickly rejected and with it the sweet, brief memory of Jesus.

Over the weeks as the heavy livestock, grain, and fresh water were depleted, the *Greyhound* was gradually relieved of the extra burden she'd set out with. And as was expected, with her reduced weight she was making good time.

By now, though, she'd been nearly two years at sea and was in poor condition. Her sails were patched and darned over and over. Fraying ropes had been spliced time and time again. In the hot African climate, her timbers above the waterline had shrunk and were now splitting and splintering, allowing the oakum padding to fall out.

On March 1, as she turned from the Newfoundland Banks, strong winds blew up at her stern, adding additional power which would hasten her homeward. Eight days later the winds had reached gale force and John Newton retired to his cabin that night to sleep soundly, with thoughts of shortly seeing England, his father—and perhaps, Polly.

He was jolted from his slumber when the ship suddenly lurched in what seemed to be several directions at once. In the next instant, water gushed into his cabin and shouts from above told him they were sinking.

Everyone swam for the ladder and as his cabin was nearest to it, John reached it first. No sooner had he set foot on the first rung when the captain appeared and began to make his way down. On seeing John he called for him to go and get a knife, then he turned and made his way back on deck.

John went off in search of a knife while the man next in line took his place and quickly scrambled up the ladder. But on reaching the top, before he could grip on to anything, another enormous wave swamped the ship and he vanished overboard.

Although the conditions alone would have prevented a rescue attempt, by then each man was fighting for his own life. The one consolation was, in those icy waters, the one lost overboard wouldn't survive more than a few seconds before blissful oblivion overtook him to be swiftly followed by death.

With this sudden change, the *Greyhound* was now heading into the wind. Water teemed into her through the gaping timbers, and mountainous waves poured over her prow. However, the stout-hearted ship with her ultra-lightweight cargo dipped and rose, climbing up fierce, vertical walls of water only to plunge down into yawning voids on the other side. Every dive threatened to be the last and she would surely continue on her downward path to the ocean bed. Each straining climb back to the surging crest ahead threatened to tip her over from prow to stern.

In the roar and confusion, orders were lost to the wind but the men knew instinctively what to do. All hands fell to the pumps but under the deluge, the pumps alone proved ineffectual, and they resorted to the pathetic system of baling with pails, pots, and pans.

Soaking wet and numbed with cold, it was by some miracle that they managed to do either. Battered by falling timbers and all manner of obstacles hurtling past, they were also being flung against the hull and the rail. Their only incentive to carry on was the knowledge that daylight was a mere 60 minutes away. Then they would see better what their situation was—if the *Greyhound* was still afloat then.

With the dawn, the winds suddenly calmed and the raging sea abated—but only slightly. Waves still washed over their heads, and whatever task the men performed, they first had to tether themselves to some solid object to avoid sharing the same fate as their luckless companion.

Under the deluge, shrunken timbers had swelled up to springing point and leaks were appearing all over the vessel. Clothing and bedding were crammed into the gaps. Over these some men nailed any pieces of timber they could find while others continued to man the pumps—a futile task when each wave more than replaced the volume of water being pumped out.

After operating one pump for nine hours, John was on the verge of collapse and staggered below where he found a bunk. Its bedding had been appropriated for filling gaps, its timbers were saturated, but at least it was above water level and he thankfully tumbled into it. An hour later he was called back on deck, but when the captain saw the state he was in, he declared him unfit to return to the pump. John suggested that to keep him upright and thus prevent him from falling into an exhausted heap, and also to keep him from being washed overboard, he should be lashed to the helm and left to steer the ship.

This being done, the captain was just walking

away when John muttered, "And if this won't do . . . the Lord have mercy on us."

Doubting what he'd heard, the captain turned and stared at him. Only then did John realize what he'd said.

For another eleven hours he steered the ship and in that time he searched his mind for an explanation. "The Lord have mercy on us!"—had he really said that, he wondered. John found himself recalling prayers from childhood, remembering his mother's words, the teachings of Isaac Watts' Catechism, and the pure goodness of Dr. Jennings. Half-forgotten scriptures poured into his confused mind. But of what use? There could be no mercy for him. And in thinking that, he accepted the existence of God. But why should the Lord suddenly enter *my* heart, *my* soul, he wondered? *Me*, John Newton, the most profane and debauched man on board?

The Book of Proverbs says, "I will mock when your fear cometh." It also says, "Then shall they call upon me but I will not answer." With those thoughts racing through his mind, John was filled with despair and terror. He was facing death and it was too late for absolution.

Then a sudden inner calm fell upon him as he recalled another line—"I have stretched out my hand." Eagerly he grasped at God's outstretched hand, at His love and His mercy. In his mind he was back in the chapel beside his mother listening to Isaac Watts. At the time he'd been more attracted to the little preacher's cheerful countenance and snow-white hair than to his words. Now those words were uppermost in his mind—"Short as the

watch that ends the night before the rising sun. . . .
Our shelter from the stormy blast and our eternal
home."

Utterly spent, he worked on, now more afraid of
death than before. What if he was wrong and only
imagined God had "stretched out His hand"—to
him, the most wretched of sinners. Again he recalled the words of Isaac Watts—"Art thou afraid
His power shall fail when comes thy evil day? Eternal are thy mercies, Lord, and let every trembling
thought be gone."

During those long hours, by degrees, the storm
subsided until, by dawn again, they were sailing
under a moderate wind but still fearful of sinking,
for the ship was a floating wreck.

When he was next relieved of his duties, John
stumbled belowdecks again and sank into the wet,
dank-smelling bunk. And though he longed to pray,
he resisted the urge. With death held slightly in
abeyance he reconsidered every minute of the previous horrendous hours. There was still that inner
calm, a glow even. But was it from the Lord or was
it self delusion? Had he been clutching out at anything for help in his final hours? He wasn't sure of
anything . . . but he longed for it to be true.

Lying there, John remembered the warm night
in the Mediterranean when he had dreamed of the
stranger who gave him a *magic* ring. Faced with
ridicule from another for believing in its powers,
he'd foolishly discarded it. When the first stranger
returned and retrieved the ring, he had promised
to keep it safe until such time as John called for it—
when he would have proved worthy of it. John wondered now if this was what the dream had foretold,

because he was now calling—praying—to have the precious ring returned.

Frozen and tired, the men were weak from their exertions. Below decks was awash. The galley was a shambles and all cooking utensils had been taken for baling purposes. The firewood was floating in water, and there was no chance of a hot meal. Only then did they realize that their entire stock had disappeared; goats, pigs, sheep, and poultry, all gone overboard together with the crates and barrels that had been roped down on deck.

The few stored in the hold were still intact but, save for the blessing of copious amounts of drinking water, the casks of flour and grain were useless on their own. After a more thorough search they discovered a case of dried salt-fish and a barrel of pig food, which should be enough to feed them for a week.

There was still no respite from the pumps, but with the waves no longer flushing over the ship they could afford to stop baling. According to their unreliable charts and general observations of the sun and the moon, they thought they were about a league—three miles—off the Outer Hebrides; an area unfrequented by ships, particularly at that time of the year, so there was no hope of assistance. In reality they were more than nine miles away in an even more remote spot than they feared.

But with the storm at an end, they were able to set course again, even though with her few remaining sails in shreds, the *Greyhound* remained at the mercy of the wind, often drifting helplessly for hours at a time.

11

Reformed

When the storm was over, John thanked
God for their deliverance and he assumed
the captain had prayed too. But he wondered by what means the others believed they'd
been saved when the elements' sole aim had been
to destroy the vessel with all hands.

Wedged on a small, high shelf in the captain's
cabin and safely kept dry were the books John had
derived so much amusement from in the early part
of the voyage. After all temporary repairs were finished he started reading them again—this time
with a different approach.

He hadn't bothered to read the New Testa-
ment—it had played such a large part of his childhood teaching that he thought it held no undiscov-
ered revelations. Now it was this he turned to,
devouring its content with the same hunger he'd
once eagerly digested the Earl of Shaftsbury's
"Characteristics." And there, just as at his mother's
knee, were the answers to all his questions and
doubts. He was close to her again and all he'd
learned from her came pouring back into his heart.

From then on, John's companions noticed a

great change in him. He became quiet and with-drawn. Never a foul word passed his lips and he flinched whenever they uttered profanities.

Eventually, on the fifth day after the storm, as daylight broke and the helmsman had just com-pleted one leg of a gentle southeast-southwest "tacking" maneuver, the watch yelled, "Land Ahoy!" Men flocked to the tattered remnants of the ship's side to look out and behold the glorious coast-line of western Ireland.

"Splice the mainbrace," was the next call to go up as the captain produced a small keg of rum from his cabin. Everyone was given a tot of the warming liquid, but even as they drank it their elation turned to horror when the land mass quickly broke up and evaporated into nothing. They were cele-brating the appearance of a mirage, a mere optical illusion.

Wild curses rent the air from all but John New-ton. And this bizarre behavior from one who, until recently, had been the most ungodly aboard caused a silence to fall among them. Then, as one person, they turned their despair and anger on to him. With one man overboard, their number was reduced from the ominous thirteen to twelve, yet the entire com-pany was convinced *he* had jinxed the ship. He'd fooled them all with trickery and sorcery. Suspi-cion, coupled with superstition, ran riot.

Even the captain, who would normally have risen above blind prejudice, said he regretted tak-ing him on board and accused him of being some sort of Jonah. Days earlier that would have been a ludicrous allegation, but now John was spiritually reborn and firmly believed in God again. His conversion had only come about because of the storm, yet he doubted God had blown it up for that purpose. Even if He had, it was too late to implore the crew to toss him over the side in the belief God would immediately calm the waters—they were already calm.

It was odd, though, how men who had never known the Lord, let alone heard of the prophet, were all of the same mind to commit that very biblical act. Among the roughest, who were formerly his confederates, there was even talk of killing and eating him.

Two days after sighting the "land" phenomenon, one man, working at the pump, collapsed and died. Over the next weeks, food was strictly rationed with *half* of one salted fish, rehydrated but uncooked, being shared daily between *all* of the men. It was quite indigestible but fortunately, with six casks still unopened, there was an almost limitless supply of drinking water—albeit stale—to help them swallow the barely edible food.

It was April, three full months from the beginning of the storm, before they sighted a true land mass: Tory Island, lying just off the northern coast of Ireland, with her lush green mountains rising toward the heavens. For a day and a night, the valiant ship struggled on toward a haven growing ever closer.

Only then did they discover their water supply wasn't as plentiful as they'd thought. On opening a *fresh* cask it was found to be empty. So was the next. Another was also empty and another and another, their backs smashed in during the storm. They'd consumed the last drop of water without anyone suspecting it. Had the discovery been made a day earlier, frustration and despair would undoubtedly have erupted, driving the men to violence—all directed against their Jonah, John.

The ragged vessel crawled into mist-bound Lough Swilly at County Donegal, Ireland, and no sooner did she drop anchor when yet another tremendous storm broke overhead. Two hours earlier, and the *Greyhound* would have been swept back out to open sea and certain destruction.

Knowing his father would be aware the ship was long overdue, following his first night ashore, John's most urgent task was to write to him. The letter wasn't merely to let him know he hadn't drowned at sea but to tell him he had reformed and to beg his forgiveness for everything he'd done in the past.

He wanted to write to Polly as well but he was afraid to. Instead, he wrote to her aunt, asking if Polly was married and if not would she write to him, in care of Mr. Manesty in Liverpool. He wrote also to his old friend, Dr. Jennings, whom he'd gladly excluded from his life and his memory these past years.

Captain Newton was overjoyed at John's letter. Assuming the ship was lost, he'd given up all hope of ever seeing him again. He'd abandoned all hope years ago of him ever returning to the fold of Christianity, and this was like the Prodigal Son returned—not only to his father but to the Lord.

He wrote back, telling John he would be welcomed home with open arms. He also told him that Thomasin had given birth to a third child. He made no reference to the annual £400 legacy that the

Greyhound's captain had promised John, which didn't surprise him at all. The letter did contain a note of sadness though.

His father was shortly leaving for Canada to work for the Hudson Bay Company. Set up over 70 years earlier to trade in furs and skins, their employees were constantly under threat from maverick traders, trappers, and native American Indians, so a series of forts had been built to defend them. It was to one of these, Fort York, that Captain Newton was taking up the post of Governor for a three-year term. Thomasin and the children were staying behind in London, but if John returned to England as soon as possible, he could accompany him to Canada as his personal assistant. This was forgiveness indeed.

Meanwhile John had found lodgings with a warm Londonderry family who were delighted to have a devout Christian boy staying with them rather than some of the loutish seafarers they'd known in the past. (If they'd met him a few weeks earlier they wouldn't have tolerated him under their roof.)

With Irish kindness and hospitality John was being nursed back to health. Every day he attended morning and evening prayers in the church and, in the privacy of his room, he fervently prayed for future guidance.

While he was in Ireland, John and his father wrote regularly to each other. In one letter, the Captain told him he'd visited the Catletts to let them know he was safe. Polly was now twenty years old but still unmarried, nor was she "promised" to anyone.

The *Greyhound* had needed extensive repairs and John felt obliged to wait and sail to England on her. But the repairs took far longer than anticipated and she didn't arrive back in Liverpool until the end of May—on the very day Captain Newton left London for Canada.

John's main priority on reaching Liverpool was to visit Joseph Manesty, firstly to thank him for his part in helping to trace him and secondly, in the hope that Polly or her aunt had replied to his letter.

But he was disappointed. Mr. Manesty received him warmly and surprised John by telling him the *Greyhound*'s captain had preempted his visit and given a glowing report of "the young man's conduct in the face of disaster." He was so impressed, he offered John command of his newest slaver, the *Brownlow*, currently being outfitted for Africa.

Naturally, John was flattered but refused on the grounds that he wasn't ready for such responsibility nor did he know enough about the slave trade. With his fresh attitude toward respecting authority he felt he had a lot to learn, so instead he offered to sail on her as First Mate. Manesty admired his honesty and gave command of the *Brownlow* to the *Greyhound*'s First Mate, who had also played a large part in saving the ship.

John was just two months from his twenty-third birthday and his new appointment provided the sort of financial backing a man needed if he were contemplating marriage. Again he wrote to Polly's aunt and a week later a reply came saying that the Catletts were presently staying in London, but she knew they would be pleased to see him. They'd also granted him permission to "pay court" to their daughter.

John immediately made enquiries about transport. A twice-weekly stagecoach to London was leaving that very afternoon from Warrington, a town fourteen miles away. Wasting no time, he hired a livery horse and rode there, arriving with barely ten minutes to spare.

It took three days to cover the 200 miles. Before going to visit Polly, he went to his father's home to see Thomasin and the children, take a bath, and brush down his dusty, travel-creased clothes. When he reached the house where the Catletts were staying, he was received as warmly as on his first visit six years earlier. But this time it was a mature and serious looking young man they welcomed rather than the swaggering braggart of the past. Polly, too, had changed. The shy and simple girl had developed into a self-assured woman who greeted him cordially, but with none of the exuberance she'd shown previously.

John was taken aback at her transformation. He felt awkward and so tongue-tied he was unable to say any of the things he'd planned. It was a complete reversal from when they'd last met when he was so arrogant and cocksure.

Another obvious change of character was when, after two hours, the young man who had once neglected his duties and overstayed every leave, announced that it was time for him to go. As he left he found the courage to ask if he might write to her. Polly's reply was a slight and dignified nod.

John stayed the night at Thomasin's before returning to Liverpool to help supervise the *Brown-*

low's preparation for sailing. The fare to London
had been £2—a First Mate's wage for *two weeks*.
When considering that a farm laborer's weekly
wage was three shillings (15p), the stage fare was
very expensive even for those times—in winter it
would have cost an extra £1. Had the Catletts been
at home rather than in London, he couldn't even
have afforded the extra twenty miles to Chatham,
so he couldn't possibly afford to take any kind of
transport back north.

Except for the occasional lift on farm carts—
which rarely took him more than a couple of
miles—he walked all the way and slept under
hedge-rows at night. His only nourishment came
from the few victuals Thomasin had packed for him
and the odd jug of ale from wayside inns.

Throughout the journey his heart was filled
with love for Polly, yet she hadn't given the least
intimation that he meant anything other than a
long-lost brother to her. Footsore and weary, he got
back to Liverpool a week later, then wrote again to
her aunt. But in that letter he poured out his un-
dying love for Polly, adding that, though he was un-
worthy of her, his heart was breaking and did she
think Polly would ever consider marrying him?

From then on he tried to put all thoughts of
Polly out of his mind and applied himself to his
work.

Preparing the *Brownlow* involved the usual
stowing of provisions and cargo John had been familiar with since childhood. What was new to him
were the additional articles, common and necessary
to slavers and slave ships. There were branding
irons, yokes, shackle irons, and all manner of hor-

rific and cruel devices intended to keep slaves oppressed. There were cases of manillas—narrow brass bangles used as currency and it took very few to purchase a human being. There were also sacks of dried pulses which, moistened with water, provided the sole tasteless diet for slaves in transit.

John didn't consider any of this brutal or distasteful. Like most people he thought the trade a highly respectable Christian pursuit, even though he personally had suffered as a slave and seen others suffer too.

Until then he'd only operated on the fringe of the trade. The ship in which he'd first sailed to Africa was only part way through her expedition when he left with Mr. Clow for the Plantain Islands. For a while there, he had been involved in the purchase of slaves and again later at Kittam. He'd also seen them at work on the islands and had them as his servants. But he knew absolutely nothing about the shipment of slaves on a large scale.

Now he was about to embark on the darkest period of his life.

When all was ready, with two days to go before sailing, a letter arrived from Polly saying she didn't care for any other, so on his return from Africa, she would *probably* marry him.

Weeping for joy, John went to his knees and thanked God for giving him a glimmer of hope, no matter how faint.

12

The Middle-Passage

The *Brownlow*, with twenty-five officers and men, was destined for the Sestro River, an area north of Sierra Leone. Once there, she would trade up and down the river for about six months, gradually filling the holds with black, human cargo.

As her captain rarely went ashore, except to meet tribal chiefs or dine with traders, John's job was similar to the one he'd had at Kittam. But here he was in strange territory with no known reputation for fair trading.

In the villages he and his men were often surrounded by natives whose attitude was, at times, positively menacing. And whenever they left the longboat to travel overland, they went well armed. From all around in the dense jungle came growls, screeches, and snarls from wild animals stalking them. They knew lions abounded in that region and they were never sure they weren't being observed by hostile tribesmen.

Despite these dangers, though, Africa soon began to weave her spell over John. First he began forgetting his evening prayers. Each day in Ireland he'd set apart some time to read the Bible. Now this too was overlooked. At night on watch, if there were no other vessels anchored close by to distract his attention, through the trees he would catch a glimpse of flickering fires and hear the throb of native drums from nearby villages. The eerie sounds of marauding beasts, the scent of luscious vegetation, and the brilliant stars lighting up a velvet black sky reminded him of the year he'd spent at Kittam, a king among men.

The colorful memories caused his heart to beat wildly. He recalled times spent in friendly, isolated villages where pagan rituals and heathen gods had seemed far more real and natural to his brutalized senses than the sweetness of his mother or the hymns of Isaac Watts. His newfound faith in the Lord slipped further and further from him until he succumbed to the lure and the laws of the jungle. God's outstretched hand was no longer necessary.

From then on he grew more insensitive to the rights, feelings, and dignity of humanity than at any time in his young life. Where some would take the trouble to walk around a prone slave, John Newton would step on the body with as little regard as he would tread on a clod of earth. He grumbled incessantly about the moaning of the sick and the screams from the tormented.

Two months after arriving in Africa the *Brownlow* reached the Plantain Islands and John was sent to do business with Mr. Clow. He was cordially greeted by both him and his wife and, in return, showed more deference to them than to the slaves who had nursed him during his terrible illness and maltreatment at Pey Ey's hands. Walking among them he returned their smiles of recognition with contempt and cold indifference.

When he was taken out to see the limes he'd been forced to plant two years earlier, he taunted his host, saying that when he returned the following year in command of his own ship, they would just be bearing their first fruit and he promised to buy some.

While their lengthy transaction was taking place, he lived in the same little house he'd once called "home" and again, with Polly as far from his mind as the Lord, he took a native wife. Then, by sheer coincidence, he fell seriously ill with the same fever as before, and the longboat, with its crew, had to return to the ship without him.

This time, however, Clow and Pey Ey nursed him well, feeding him the most delicate fare and ample supplies of water and lime juice. Yet, in his delirium, especially whenever Pey Ey visited him with some native, medicinal potion, he believed he was still at her mercy. He was lying on a wooden case in the shabby hut with a log of wood for a pillow with the princess towering over him, laughing and refusing him water.

He was so ill, death seemed inevitable, and in his more lucid moments he realized how far he'd traveled down the road from God's merciful deliverance. Surely it would have been better if the crew on the *Greyhound* had tossed him overboard or even killed and eaten him as they'd threatened to.

Hallucinating, he saw Jesus on the cross— where he personally had put Him to be crucified all over again. He questioned the degree of mercy and forgiveness the Lord could give and decided there was no mercy now, nor should there be, for such a sinner.

Yet, wasn't the Lord's mercy endless, he reasoned? So in every waking minute he prayed as he had never prayed before, not even when he was in danger of drowning. For this, after being returned to the Lord and forsaking Him again was worse than drowning.

Almost at once he began to recover. As his strength returned, he would sneak out at night to the cave on the shore where he had once drawn geometrical diagrams. This time though, he groveled on the ground, begging God for mercy and forgiveness. He promised to give up his tribal wife and cast all thoughts of pagan ritual from his mind.

Eventually, he was fully recovered and Clow personally escorted him back to the *Brownlow*. From that time, whenever John went ashore, he wandered into the jungle, not to satisfy a lusting for heathen practices, exciting dances or wild, rhythmic drumbeats but because, among the trees, he felt closer to God than anywhere else.

He began reading Bible passages again and resumed his Latin studies.

In the week before sailing for the Middle-Passage, he was put in charge of a "wooding and water" party—collecting firewood for cooking and drinking water for storage in casks. This work lasted eight nights and could only be done after the general day's chores were finished. With just one more loading to complete, John was about to set off in the longboat to join the party upriver when the captain called him back to ask him something, and sent the Second Mate instead. Next morning, they discovered the longboat had sunk in mid-river and the Second Mate had drowned. John felt sure the fate should have been his.

At last the ship was fully loaded, by which time the first slaves to be bought had been on board for almost a year.

Some slave ships were converted whalers while others, like the *Brownlow*, were built specifically for the trade, but they were all modeled on the same lines. The headroom belowdecks was no more than five feet, forcing everyone except the smallest to walk around bent double. The sides were lined with tiers of shelves on which lay the slaves. Men, women, and children were put in separate compartments, but while the men were always chained together in pairs, women were rarely tied up and children never.

Previously, John had only seen them "loose-packed"—lying on their backs—which afforded some space to move or turn. But on board the *Brownlow* they were "spoon-packed"—lying on their sides—a position that allowed not an inch of space between.

More tiers stood in rows stretching the length of the lower deck with only narrow aisles for walking along. When ledges were so tightly packed that slaves would fall off if more were put there, a crewman was sent down to ensure *more were put there*. The atmosphere was hot and so airless that candles were unable to burn, so everywhere was in constant darkness. Eventually, when no more could be pushed into the already stinking hold, the ship set sail on the Middle-Passage for a four-month voyage to Antigua in the West Indies. Upon arrival the slaves were sold, and the holds thoroughly cleaned out and refilled with a cargo of sugar, rum, tea, coffee, indigo dye, and tobacco.

With fresh merchandise the ship would return to England, unload, then reload with textiles, machinery, muskets, manillas, cheap ornaments and trinkets, and set off for Africa and the Triangular Trade all over again.

The air was rent with groans from the sick and dying. Every morning dead slaves were found, chained to their living companions, where they remained until it was convenient for the corpses to be removed. Then they were flung overboard like ship's refuse. In those conditions, with all their tribal superstitions, some slaves went insane and became as violent as was possible in the confined space. On some ships, slaves who were merely sick were thrown overboard to the sharks. Invariably this was regarded as a bonus by the "cargo," since it gave some extra space and helped relieve the excruciating pain they suffered by being so cramped.

Women, packed tightly together, gave birth to babies and then, literally unable to move, were unable to tend them. Happily for the infants, they rarely survived more than a few hours—then they too were tossed overboard.

The near-naked slaves lay in their own urine, excrement, and vomit. Officers walked among them with small bags of camphor clasped to their noses to offset the revolting stench. John complained at the constant putrid stench in his nostrils and at having to be on board with the most unclean creatures he had ever known. It didn't occur to him that the fault wasn't theirs.

The hitherto proud Africans were humiliated in other ways too. On fine days, they were taken up on deck in small groups where, to the accompaniment of a drum, they were forced, under the frequent lash from a cat o' nine tails, to execute wild dances and sing. This was claimed to give them exercise and keep them fit and healthy but was really a form of entertainment for the crew.

Some were terrified of the vast ocean with never a sight of land, while others, particularly those who had been imprisoned for a year by that time, were quite clearly demented. After being at sea for two months, one day a group of slaves, while on deck for air, suddenly went berserk. Before the ship's company could be alerted one crewman had been murdered. Alarm bells rang throughout the ship and everyone raced on deck. Within minutes the attack was quelled with four slaves killed and others injured. Their injuries didn't prevent them from being sentenced to be flogged to "within an inch of their life" though. And they were the fortunate ones. The worst offenders were put to the thumbscrews; a method of torture whereby the thumbs were placed in a vice whose screw was then turned until the joint fractured and the flesh burst open. The operation could last hours or *days* depending on the speed of turning.

There had been no logic to the slaves uprising, for the *Brownlow* was in mid-Atlantic and had it succeeded none of them knew how to sail a huge ship like a Guineaman. They were only used to rowing primitive canoes.

Approaching Antigua, the slaves were told they were nearing the end of the voyage. They were unchained and taken on deck where they were hosed down and the men shaved. Afterwards they were given olive oil and beeswax to rub their bodies with in order to make their black skin shine like silk.

Naively believing their ordeal was finally over, they expected to be released, little knowing the worst was yet to come. All the care and attention was to make them more attractive to potential purchasers. From there on they faced a life of relentless hard work, floggings, starvation, and all sorts of abuse and cruelties.

Sadly, in this instance, instead of being delivered to Joseph Manesty's agent, he told them the prices were down in the Antigua marketplace and they must sail on—almost two thousand miles—to Charleston, Carolina, a southeast state of North America.

Herded back into the hold and being chained up again, the "cargo" realized the voyage was continuing. Not understanding their new destination or how long it would take, some of the poor wretches went mad and murdered their companions.

The *Brownlow* had set out from Africa with 218 slaves, of whom 62 died on the Middle-Passage. But this was a "good" ship. Usually there were approximately 500 men, women, and children in a cargo, but the death rate was always expected to be around twenty percent.

At Charleston, John soon learned about the three different sales methods: top-grade slaves— the fittest and strongest—were taken to "factories" where prospective owners or their agents inspected them before purchasing. Sometimes orders for specific types were sent in advance. These high-quality "goods" could bring as much as £100 each.

The second method was by "scramble"—the most sordid of all. Potential buyers lined up on the quayside while the slaves were brought up from the hold; all males—children included—were put on the foredeck, all females on the quarterdeck. After a tarpaulin sheet was thrown over them to obliterate all light, a signal was given and buyers "scrambled" aboard to grab as many terrified slaves as they could. These slaves went at a bargain price of £28 each.

The auction block was the usual method, though, yet it was mostly the old, weak, and sickly who went there at a knock-down price of £1 each. Incredibly, it was often the more compassionate members of society who bought them. While failing to acknowledge that slavery in itself was immoral and sinful, they at least tried to keep families together. The sick were nursed back to health and were so grateful they were loyal to their owners for the rest of their lives.

Quite unmoved, John frequently watched entire families being wrenched apart to be sold separately for various uses—men, teenage boys, and robust women for work on the land, and other women and children for domestic service or factory work. Those taken into domestic service were nearly always treated well—even with affection—by the families they served. Nevertheless they were prisoners, abducted from their own land, and had neither rights nor freedom.

Sadly all of this had no more effect on John's conscience than if he'd been to a cattle market.

13

In Command

*I*t took four months to fumigate and scour the ship, then reload her with provisions and a cargo. As they had been diverted from the West Indies to the American mainland this was made up of tobacco, cotton, and rice rather than the expected rum, sugar, tea, and coffee.

After being absent for over a year, in the week before Christmas 1749, the *Brownlow* slipped back into her berth in the River Mersey at Liverpool. Assured by her captain that the First Mate had given a good account of himself, Manesty immediately offered John a command on the next ship leaving for Africa. This could be months ahead, though, as all his ships, other than the *Brownlow*, were at sea.

Despite the misery, tragedy, filth, and death he'd encountered, John couldn't wait to embark on the Triangular Trade again. Furthermore, he felt confident and experienced enough to become a fully qualified slaver, so he accepted the command.

His one thought after that was to write and tell Polly he was home and would soon be coming to see her. When he arrived in Kent a week later, though, she received him even more coolly than on his last visit. He'd taken her an expensive, beautifully bound prayer book but the gift didn't impress her. Nevertheless, in spite of her aloofness, remembering what she'd said in her letter before he sailed for Africa, as soon as they were alone, John asked her to marry him. But not only did Polly refuse, she forbade him ever to ask her again.

Distraught, he rushed out to the woods behind the house where he fell to his knees and prayed. Was this the Lord's punishment for falling under the hypnotic charms of the dark continent again, he asked? But he found no solace in prayer, so he wandered along to Polly's aunt's house to seek her advice. She was dismayed at her niece's rejection and urged him to ask her again.

Elizabeth and George Catlett, who by now fully approved of John, couldn't understand their daughter's change of heart either. They told him she'd actually spoken of the time when she would be married to him. This gave John renewed hope and he proposed again, and again, and again. Still Polly refused—but each time a little less adamantly.

Eventually, she confessed she was afraid to marry him. After all, they didn't know each other well. Furthermore, he would be away at sea for maybe years at a time while she was left ashore, living in strange places, knowing no one.

Her parents tried to help by suggesting she stay with them while he was away but to no avail. Eventually, Polly admitted her real reason for declining John's proposal. She didn't trust him because of his past reckless behavior.

It took a lot of persuading to convince her he'd changed, but finally her real self emerged and she was once more the warmhearted, happy, fun-loving girl he'd first fallen in love with. A fortnight later, in February 1750, at Rochester in Kent, they were married.

From then on John rarely heard his name spoken, for Polly always addressed him as "dearest," "my dear," or "dear heart." He'd never known such affection since he was a child. His only regret was she didn't share his love for God.

Although Polly was a Christian and attended church regularly, she didn't feel any deep commitment to the Lord. For some time, John had made a practice of kneeling to pray each night before he got into bed, but now he felt too embarrassed to pray in front of her. Consequently he felt guilty for not doing so.

With his newfound happiness, he wasn't looking forward to taking his own command anymore—or even going back to sea. He wanted to settle ashore and tried finding suitable employment with a similar wage to that of ship's master. He took to gambling in lotteries, hoping to *win* enough money to enable him to stay at home but every ticket was a loser. He even borrowed to pursue the vice, but still lost and ended up owing £70.

At last, in the first week of May, when they'd been married three months, the letter he'd been dreading arrived. He was summoned back to the north of England to take up his command. He left Chatham on the eighteenth and, not knowing if it would be one or two years before they met again, the heartbroken pair said their tearful farewells.

Back in Liverpool, however, the ship he was to captain had returned badly storm damaged. It could be weeks before she was seaworthy again or before an alternative vessel was available. Due to bad weather, they were all either overdue or arriving back in a sorry state. Meanwhile, Mr. Manesty had business in London he needed someone to attend to. John seemed the obvious candidate as he could return to Kent and stay a further ten days.

He hired a sturdy horse for the journey and, all the way, he kept remembering a similar errand when he was seventeen and preparing to leave for Jamaica but stayed at the Catletts' instead. What odd turns his life had taken since then.

Polly had wept bitterly when her husband left for Liverpool and couldn't believe he was back so soon. Yet, ironically, his return almost caused their final separation. Riding back at the end of his leave, he was within a couple of miles of Liverpool when he noticed his horse was thirsty. There was a pond beside the track, so he urged his mount on to what he thought was the shallow water's edge—only to tumble headlong into deep water.

Horse and rider struggled out and, except for the discomfort of cold, wet clothes, John thought nothing of the incident until he stopped at the next Inn to get dry. There he discovered he'd fallen not into a pool, but a flooded clay pit where three people had drowned that week.

Arriving in Liverpool he learned that his ship was nearing completion of her refit. Although the *Duke of Argyle* wasn't a big Guineaman, as he'd expected, but a much smaller, 140-ton, three-masted Snow, he was so pleased at getting his own ship all ideas of settling ashore fled.

Three weeks after his twenty-fifth birthday,

young Captain Newton took command of what soon transpired to be a decrepit old ship in little better condition than the *Greyhound* had been after two years at sea. But all the same, he was proud at attaining the same lofty position and authority his father had enjoyed, so proud in fact that he began reflecting his every characteristic.

Just as he was never permitted to laugh until his father laughed first, he forbade anyone within his hearing to say what time it was until they'd first conferred with him. No one was allowed to eat until he gave permission to do so. He demanded a ceremonial send-off whenever he left the ship, and men had to keep a keen lookout in order to give him a formal welcome when he returned. No man could retire to his hammock until then. Still, he was considerate of them and always got back at a reasonable hour.

John had bought a large, 450-page, leatherbound book in which he intended listing every single aspect of life at sea. On the first evening, after dining with his officers, he retired to his cabin, sat down, and opened the book to make his first entry. The opening page, written mostly in Latin, read:

Praise be to God
Journal kept on board Duke of Argyle
Snow from Liverpool to Africa
Commenced August 14, 1750.

This entry was followed by an extract from Psalm 107:

They that go down to the sea in ships
That do business in great waters

These see the works of the Lord
and His wonders in the deep.

At the bottom of the page he entered a quote from the Roman poet Horace to the effect that the journal would be a nice keepsake to read in his declining years.

Unlike other ranks, John had a lot of leisure time, so he read Latin classics and love poems which he then translated into English and dedicated to God—and to Polly. Every day he read the Bible. Saturday evenings he considered as part of the Sabbath. Each Sunday he rose at 4:00 A.M. and walked the deck, meditated, then returned to his cabin to read two or three chapters from the Bible. He ate his breakfast in complete silence and followed it with more prayers. At 11:00 A.M. the ship's bell called the crew to morning service, conducted by John. In the afternoon there were more prayers. After tea in his cabin at 4:00 P.M., the crew was called on deck for a scripture lesson. After this he walked the deck again, meditating. At 6:00 P.M. he retired to his cabin for private prayers.

This procedure took place no matter where they were, what was happening, and regardless of weather conditions. The crew could barely disguise their resentment at all this piety. And their lack of religion worried the captain. Overlooking his own former lack of reverence despite being well educated, he felt sure it was illiteracy that fostered their atheism. They didn't understand the Bible or the formal prayers he recited at the services.

That prompted him to write to Dr. Jennings asking him to compile a simple book of prayers for sailors, of which John promised to buy a hundred copies and assured him all other captains would buy them too.

The letter, together with some to Polly and his father, was put on the first ship they met heading for the Middle-Passage, and eventually England.

As much as he liked his work, how John missed Polly—especially when faced with problem after problem. The First and Second Mates and the ship's doctor always gave him their full support. But, with the exception of those three, that ship was crewed by the worst bunch of scoundrels John had ever known. Their crudeness, drunkenness, profanities, lewd songs, and foul language—all once his favorite sports—sickened him. Rumors of mutiny were forever circulating around the ship and, on reaching his ears, John didn't hesitate to order floggings.

Four of the most degenerate got involved in far worse escapades than John had ever dreamed of at his most disruptive. One, Will Lees, refused to go on watch at night and threatened the Bosun with violence when he ordered him to. The Bosun himself was a rebel who frequently needed to be put in irons.

Another night, Lees and his companions slipped away in the longboat when some men from a French schooner moored nearby invited them aboard. Everyone got drunk, then Lees and his pals started a fight. Overwhelmed by the entire French crew, they attempted to escape and leaped into the longboat to get back to their own ship. Being so drunk they ran it onto rocks, and the following morning John, who should have been going in the boat to view some slaves, was stranded on board ship while the

French captain went ashore and bought them.

Their penalty for that fiasco was to be stripped and lain across a gun barrel while John personally thrashed them with a cane, then clamped them in irons for a few days.

Among the first of John's calls was a visit to the Plantain Islands, where Mr. Clow and Pey Ey again treated him with the greatest respect. Again he showed none of the animosity he'd felt as their slave. He even invited them to dinner on board. He next asked to see the lime grove where the trees were in fruit for the first time and he bought almost the entire crop. He also bought a young black sister and brother from them.

Lees was one of his rowers and when John was ready to leave the island, he was missing. A thorough search was made until he was discovered hiding in a cove, fighting drunk. Clow's slaves helped restrain him and bundled him, in irons, into the bottom of the boat.

The evening Mr. Clow and Pey Ey dined with John on the *Duke of Argyle*, Will Lees was on watch and recognized among their rowers one of the slaves who'd helped apprehend him. He struck out at him with a metal tool but missed. At this, Pey Ey turned nasty and made an awful fuss about her favorite *servant* almost being killed. And John, feeling acutely embarrassed, didn't know what to do so he gave her a lace hat from his bartering store by way of compensation.

For humiliating him in front of his former enemy, John kept Lees in irons on deck under the hot sun for four days. When he was released, John heard he and his followers were planning to mutiny.

By then he'd had enough and decided to put them on the first Royal Navy vessel he saw in exchange for three pressed men.

The weather was atrocious, with high winds and driving rain causing perilous rough seas. As usual, there were several other ships in the vicinity but all of them were merchant vessels. For hours, unknown to the rebels, the "lookout" searched through the blinding spray for a man-of-war until, at last, the *HMS Surprise* was spotted sheltering in the Sierra Leone estuary.

The *Duke of Argyle* pulled alongside and Captain Newton crossed over in the longboat. Captain Baird of the *HMS Surprise* was sympathetic and agreed to exchange the rebels for three of his own pressed men—all grateful for their release.

John's problems still weren't over, though. A feverish sailor started rambling about a mutiny planned for when they were in the Middle-Passage. All officers would be slain, the mutineers would take over and, posing as officers, sail to a port where the ship was unknown and sell the slaves for their own profit.

Lying awake late at night in his cabin, John wondered: was all this vexation the retribution from the Lord he'd been expecting for so long? Or was it nothing more than the sort of harassment most captains faced from time to time?

14

An Echo From the Past

John still believed he was engaged in a genteel occupation, but for some reason he couldn't understand, he was beginning to feel concern over slaves being maltreated. He personally examined each one brought aboard and only the fittest was kept. The sick, elderly, or feeble were returned to shore. Children came under the closest scrutiny. None under four feet in height were ever purchased.

A sample entry in his journal read:

No. 22 one boy, four feet
Nos. 24–26 three small girls (undersized)

He strictly forbade his men to abuse the slaves in any way. When one sailor was caught attacking a heavily pregnant woman, John had him put in irons and threatened with a flogging if anything happened to either the woman or her unborn baby.

Every Sunday he conducted a Christian service for them, which was neither understood nor appreciated. Belowdecks, he didn't have slaves packed as tightly as in most ships. Consequently, he didn't carry as many. Also, while the slaves were on deck for air each day, he ordered the holds to be hosed out. This wasn't so much an observation of hygiene, but rather because he couldn't stomach the nauseating smells arising from the holds when they were unbattened.

On a bitterly cold day in mid-Atlantic, when the slaves shivered from the cold, Captain Newton had them sent belowdecks again, only to avoid losing more to illness than was normal. When four slaves did die he changed the diet from black beans to rice; a more expensive commodity, but effective in curing the sickness threatening to sweep through the entire "cargo."

Nevertheless, slaves caught in the act or merely showing signs of rebellion were severely dealt with. One day, a young slave, who had always behaved so well he'd never been tied up, smuggled a marlin spike—used for separating rope strands—down into the hold. Before it was missed, twenty had pried open their chains. A few minutes more, and enough would have been freed to overcome the crew.

As the ship was running in a gale at the time, there was nothing John could do other than stand two armed guards over them right through the night. It was late the following morning before the winds calmed and they could be dealt with. The punishment was a flogging, while the ringleader was also clamped in irons and given a slight turn on the thumbscrews.

With unreliable charts and erratic compasses, no mariner was ever sure of his precise whereabouts, so it was with enormous relief that they spotted floating seaweed, indicating they were nearing land.

At Antigua, the cargo would be unloaded, the ship made ready to sail again with fresh cargo and they would be homeward bound. John so looked forward to getting home to his adored wife. And also to see his father who was due to reach England before him as his three-year contract with the Hudson Bay Company had expired.

When the *Duke of Argyle* berthed at Antigua on July 3, 1751, John could barely wait to read the package of mail waiting for him. There were letters from Polly, his father, and Dr. Jennings. There was also one from his stepmother, Thomasin, telling him his father was dead. He'd drowned after getting a cramp while swimming in the Hudson River just four days before he should have left Canada.

John was overcome with grief. He'd always held the Captain in awe yet had never really known him. However, over the past three years, although half a world apart, through their letters they had drawn closer; and just when the future seemed so promising, he was gone.

Fortunately, there was a lot of business that needed attending to, so John was kept from brooding too much on his father's death. During the voyage, six of his crew had died from fevers. This was a normal loss on any ship. The remarkable thing was, *there were only six fewer slaves than when she started out*, which was most unusual.

Some ship's masters, astonished at this, commended John on his successful voyage, especially his first as a captain. Others scoffed at his odd methods, pointing out he could have risked working at a loss and that wouldn't be appreciated by the owner, Joseph Manesty, or his shareholders.

The next evening, when dining with Manesty's agent, he also questioned the wisdom of John's ways. Wasn't it better to stack as many as possible on board, even though it might increase the death rate? After all, slaves were cheap enough to afford losing if more were shipped in the first place.

John's arrival back in England was a mixture of happiness at being reunited with Polly and sadness over his father not being there when he went to see Thomasin, now widowed with three children, ages sixteen, eight, and five.

In Liverpool, John had been told he was getting a new ship, the *African*. As she was still in the process of being built it gave him a longer leave than usual, lasting from September until April.

Pleased though he was at commanding a brand-new vessel, the prospect of leaving Polly made him more miserable than the last time. On the evening of his departure from Chatham, he sat on the edge of the bed looking thoroughly glum. Although she hadn't shown any interest, much of his leave time had been spent reading the Bible and other religious books. Now, Polly amazed him by suggesting they kneel down and pray together for his safe and speedy return.

John could scarcely believe she was placing her trust in the Lord. From then on, he knew they shared more than an earthly love and he left for Liverpool with an inner calmness and a fresh interest in his work.

Knowing Polly would be praying for him inspired him to follow an age-old practice of sailors.

He put up notices in the local churches asking the congregation to pray for his ship's safe return.

The *African*, a Guineaman, being a modern ship, had four extra inches of headroom below decks making for greater comfort for even the tallest on board. On the first leg of the voyage, remembering the terror when the slaves nearly escaped on the *Duke of Argyle*, John asked the carpenter to erect a *barricado* in their quarters. This was a stout, wooden wall, topped with metal spikes, stretching right across the slaves' "rooms," completely cutting them off from the rest of the ship. At intervals along its length were holes where guns pointed inward at the poor wretches on the far side of the wall. Thus, if any slave managed to get free of his chains he was still held secure.

The voyage involved all the usual perils and frustrations—appalling weather, difficult crew, plotting slaves, fear of mutiny—and even an attempted kidnapping by a corrupt trader claiming John had cheated him, but who was later proved to be lying.

In his letters home, feeling none of his old inhibitions, John was able to tell his wife what God meant to him; of how He'd changed him and saved his soul. Apart from Dr. Jennings, she was the first person since his mother that he'd been able to discuss such personal emotions with and, though they were parted, their love grew all the stronger for it.

He sensed he was changing even more in his attitude toward the slaves, too. Although he held the Sunday services for them, they'd never been a part of his personal prayers. But now, each night, he prayed for their souls. Until then it hadn't occurred to him that slaves had souls. He even began making the Sabbath a comparatively easy day for his crew as well.

Ships newly out from England deposited mail at the trading posts along the coast. And, just before leaving for the Middle-Passage, John received a letter telling him there was a surfeit of slaves in the market at Antigua, and to take his cargo sixty miles farther on to St. Christopher—now called St. Kitts.

The *African* was carrying 174 slaves, of whom 28 died on the Middle-Passage. This was in spite of John's unloading the troublesome and noisy ones onto a passing London-bound non-slaver, telling the captain to sell them and keep the profit for himself. After that, those remaining settled down quite happily. He noted in his journal that they were so pleasant and well-behaved, he preferred them to some of his crew.

Sickness was rife, however, and his first order on reaching St. Kitts was to have all the ship's deck and walls scraped, washed down with vinegar, then fumigated with smoking brimstone and tobacco.

His next consideration was to collect his mail, but save for one letter from Dr. Jennings there was nothing from Polly. John was frantic with worry. It meant only one of two things, she was either desperately ill or she was dead. He'd lost his father at the very time they'd established a close relationship. Was Polly now lost to him at a time when they seemed even closer through their mutual love and trust in God?

Mr. Manesty's agent on the island, Francis Guichard, and his wife did everything to cheer him up, suggesting there would have been a letter from her parents if anything had happened. But John was inconsolable.

A week later, Mr. Guichard went over to Antigua on business only to return with a sheaf of letters from Polly, who had evidently not received John's letter telling her he was going to St. Kitts. He was overwhelmed with relief and some weeks later when he set off for England he took baskets of exotic fruits and other gifts for her. At sea, while writing his journal or reading the Bible his mind wandered to Polly, reflecting on how he'd suffered when he thought he'd lost her. How was he ever going to leave her again, he wondered.

He arrived back fourteen months after setting out and went post haste to Chatham, where he persuaded Polly to go north with him so they could spend all of his leave together while he was preparing the *African* for her next trip. They rented some comfortable rooms in Liverpool and spent their evenings wandering along the banks of the Mersey or walking in the woods and beautiful Lancashire countryside.

It was while waiting for his ship that John bumped into someone whose existence he'd almost forgotten: Job Lewis, the young midshipman from aboard the *HMS Harwich*. A merchant captain himself by then, Job was waiting for a new ship, a Guineaman, and his first voyage to the slave coast. And, as he knew little about the slave trade, John was happy to tell him all he knew. He wasn't happy to learn that Job had developed into a heavy drinker, blasphemer, and atheist.

Expecting to be commended, Job boasted about his evil way of life. He couldn't believe it when John expressed horror at his revelations. John knew he was personally responsible for Job's downfall and determined right then to reverse what he'd so easily achieved on board the *HMS Harwich*.

But Job's conversion to sin was total. It was as though he'd not only rejected the Lord, he'd willingly given his soul into the devil's charge. When his former tutor told him how he'd rediscovered God and righteousness, Job Lewis laughed at him. It was only the fear of death on board the *Greyhound* that had forced him to reach out to God for salvation, he scoffed. On the point of death anyone would. It was sheer luck that saved John, not divine providence.

John partially agreed with him regarding a dying man reaching out for support, but he questioned why the Lord had remained with him ever since, and why every day his convictions grew stronger. Job merely shrugged this off with some obscene comment.

He was due to sail some weeks ahead of John, but before his ship was ready the owners lost all their money, went out of business, and subsequently, Captain Lewis lost his command. Had John even suspected such a thing was possible he would have prayed for it. He went directly to his employer with a proposition—if he took Job to Africa with him to learn the trade, would he consider offering him a command on one of his ships on their return?

Joseph Manesty agreed, adding, to John's surprise and delight, that he wanted the *African* to reach St. Kitts by the following April, a mere six months from the outset—the shortest voyage he'd ever embarked upon. He should be home with Polly again within the year. Even so, it gave him months with Job, and surely by his example, in that time, his soul could be won back to God. His corruption couldn't have gone so deep as to be beyond recovery, he believed.

In October, Polly went back to Kent and, on the 21st, John set out on his fifth voyage to the West Coast of Africa. Once at sea he learned the precise depths of Job's depravity, profanity, crudeness, and disobedience, and he believed this specter from his past was finally the retribution he so richly deserved. It hadn't been Polly's refusal to marry him or the vexations of difficult crews, slaves, weather or sickness but the reappearance of Job Lewis, whose youthful goodness and trust he'd systematically destroyed for his own sadistic satisfaction, that was the Lord's plan to haunt him with memories of his own evil past, he believed.

He went over all the trouble he had caused in his youth and wished it could be undone. But it was too late now. Was it too late for Job Lewis? He wondered.

Every effort to reconcile him to God was ridiculed and seemed to drive him to further mischief. Simply to annoy John, he inveigled two officers to break into a large cask of ale and distribute it among the crew. When they were caught, Job denied any involvement but the officers were flogged with the cat o' nine tails. Next he got someone to steal a case of snuff from the hold, which he then sold to the crew. And he constantly incited them to disobey orders.

John was rapidly becoming disenchanted with

what had once been a joyous and fulfilling occupation. The sickness, odors, hostility, uncooperative crews, animosity from traders, and an ever-present fear of shipwreck were all growing tiresome.

Before he was part way to Africa, he found himself really hating everything about slaving. He didn't for one minute think there was anything ignoble about the trade though. The fault lay entirely within himself.

15

A Wretch Like Me

The *African* arrived at the Sherbro River in December and dropped anchor next to a Snow, the *Racehorse*. When the watch noticed she was completely unmanned, John made enquiries at the traders' fort on shore and learned the entire ship's company had been murdered. The ship was up for sale and, being in a terrible condition, was going at a very low price. This gave John an idea, so he bought it, then amassed a temporary crew from the fort.

If Joseph Manesty expected him to reach St. Kitts by April, by the time the *African* sailed for the Middle-Passage, her hold would be half-filled with slaves, yet still half-full of goods for barter. If, however, he left Job Lewis in command of the *Racehorse*, he could get rid of the merchandise for him and stock up with slaves ready for John's ship returning from England in less than a year's time.

Job eagerly agreed to the plan but, although he gave every indication he would carry out his duty, John left his own First Mate, Mr. Taylor, behind to help.

The *African* was leaving to trade farther down

the coast and John promised to call on the way back, both to collect Mr. Taylor and to ensure all was well before heading for the Middle-Passage. However, ten days later, as his ship sailed into the Sherbro River basin and the *Racehorse* came into view, even with his poor eyesight, Captain Newton could see her colors flying at half-mast, heralding that the ship's master was dead. When they were greeted by a series of gunshots he feared the crew had mutinied. Yet if they were dissatisfied, all they needed to do was leave the ship and return to their work on shore. As his longboat neared the ship though, it was obvious everything was in order when he was hailed by Mr. Taylor.

As soon as the *African* was out of sight, John was told, Captain Lewis had embarked on a spree of drinking and terrorism. Slaves brought on board were subjected to violence and cold-blooded cruelty. Officers and crew had become fearful of him and weren't sorry when fever struck him down and he couldn't rampage through the ship any longer. He had died three days later and was buried where the ship rode at anchor.

Job's end had been horrifying with him screaming oaths and claiming he could see the devil who had come to take his soul straight to hell. John asked if he'd prayed at all to ask for God's mercy. But he was assured he'd made no attempt to repent of his evil ways. Thus Job's own predictions were proved wrong. In the face of death he hadn't clutched at a last hope. There was no hope—no faith. All was lost.

John knelt and prayed for the soul of his former friend. He also thanked the Lord for saving him from his own evil ways. But he was curious to know why it was *he* who had been saved when he was personally responsible for demolishing all the goodness and faith in Job Lewis.

After only six weeks, instead of the usual six months on the coast and with only 87 slaves on board, John left Mr. Taylor as acting captain on the *Racehorse* and sailed for the Middle-Passage. In mid-Atlantic, he suddenly fell dangerously ill. And when he asked, the doctor told him honestly, there was no hope of recovery.

Contrary to Job's horrors of hell, John accepted his fate with serenity. If it was God's will, then so be it. His only regrets were leaving his beloved Polly and failing to rescue Job from the abyss he'd surely sent him to.

As his temperature soared, he lapsed into unconsciousness and, believing the end was near, murmured, "The Lord knoweth them that are His." Within hours, though, the fever broke and he slowly emerged from oblivion. By the time they sailed into St. Kitts in April, he was almost fully recovered. It had been the shortest voyage ever and without the death of one single slave.

Still extremely weak, John rarely ventured ashore but sat on deck, meditating on God's strange ways and wishing he understood more.

One evening he was persuaded to attend a dinner party at Francis Guichard's house where he met Alex Clunie, captain of a ship moored close to his own. In all his years at sea, this was John's first encounter with anyone whose faith was as strong as his own—save for the young Job Lewis.

For hours the two men discoursed on religion

and Alex cleared up some mysteries that were confounding John. Since Job's terrible death, he'd been worrying for fear he'd lose God again and lapse into his old ways. Alex explained that, in the past, he had deliberately shut God out of his life. But God couldn't be *lost*, just sometimes ignored for "Lo, I am with you always." He said he should talk to Him as he would to a friend, not simply through formal prayer.

Alex also spoke sadly of the lack of religion in England. He lived in London, close to where John was born, and knew both Dr. Jennings and Isaac Watts. They reminisced on the stirring sermons they used to give but Alex said, apart from Samuel Brewer, minister at his own church, present-day preachers were quite ineffective. Their dull apathy was turning people away from the churches.

There were some though who roused people's spirits. Two of these were John Wesley from Lincolnshire and George Whitefield from Gloucestershire, who traveled all over America and Britain, preaching in the open air or in sheds. Their sincere faith was attracting thousands to their meetings. They didn't belong to either the established church or the Dissenters. Some called them Reformers or Evangelists while others called them Methodists.

John was fascinated and said he would like to hear them. Alex was leaving St. Kitts before John, so he gave him Samuel Brewer's address and told him to visit him when he was in London next.

The *African* sailed for England on June 20, 1754, but because she ran into a terrible storm, the voyage took seven weeks. She reached Liverpool in August, a little over nine months from when she left. Financially it hadn't been a successful voyage, but as John left the ship he entered in his journal: *Soli Deo Gloria*. "Give all the glory to God."

A disappointment from being launched, the unreliable *African* had barely weathered the storm they'd encountered. To compensate for this, Joseph Manesty promised John his latest ship. Her keel had only just been laid, so he gave him the privilege of naming her himself, which he promptly did at first sight: *The Bee*.

It would be months before she was finished, then she would have to be loaded and generally prepared for her maiden voyage, so once more Polly came north and they rented the same rooms as before.

John regularly went to see his new ship but secretly dreaded her completion. The thought of another voyage was constantly on his mind and he couldn't sleep. As every day took him closer to leaving for another nauseating venture he felt physically and mentally sick. He was edgy and couldn't concentrate on anything.

At last, their final evening together came. Polly was packed ready for her journey back to Kent and they were sitting on the sofa in their parlor, drinking tea, when John suddenly collapsed and fell on the floor. Polly thought he was dead and cried out. The landlady came running with the maid and together they struggled to get him on to the sofa, then sent for the doctor. It was over an hour before John came around and was diagnosed as having had an apoplectic fit.

Over the next days he suffered bouts of giddiness, severe headaches, and his vision kept going out of focus. Eventually, his doctor sent for a second opinion. After examining John closely the new doctor declared the seizure was a direct result of the hot African climate and advised him never to return.

After nine years in the trade, at the age of thirty, John was forced to retire and thanked the Lord for His intervention. He'd earned enough over the years to afford a long holiday and left for Kent with a promise from Joseph Manesty that, when he was well again, he would find him alternative employment.

Back at Chatham, in the aftermath of John's collapse, Polly fell ill herself from delayed shock and appeared to be wasting away before his eyes. How John prayed for her recovery. She couldn't leave him *now* just when they were facing life together with no more separations.

Every day he sat beside her bed, spending the time studying Latin, mathematics, and perfecting the French he'd picked up on the slave coast. On fine days he wandered through the woods with his Bible in his hand. He often went to church, only to agree with what Alex Clunie had told him—the preachers were uninspiring. Every Sabbath saw him attending a different church, always with the same dissatisfaction.

One day while in London on business he called on Samuel Brewer and told him about meeting Alex and of their long talks about the itinerant evangelist preachers. As one of them, George Whitefield, was presently in London, the minister gave him a letter of introduction and John hastened along to meet him.

A jolly man with a roaring laugh, Whitefield told him he was preaching the following day and gave him a ticket to ensure entry to Whitefield's Tabernacle. The Tabernacle turned out to be a huge barn and he soon understood the need for tickets. So many hundreds came to the meeting they spilled over into the yard.

That night, John returned to Chatham with renewed faith in preachers and marveled at Whitefield's power of rhetoric.

Polly's health continued to deteriorate, so he took her to London to consult the best doctors. This proved very expensive and John knew he must find work soon. Within days a letter came from Joseph Manesty telling him of a vacancy for a Tide Surveyor in Customs and Excise at Liverpool.

John was torn between the thought of leaving Polly, who was obviously dying, and the necessity to earn money for her costly treatment if she could possibly be saved. Loving her as he did, there was no choice. Her treatment was the main consideration so, with heavy heart, he accepted the post and went back up north.

He was given a comfortable office with 55 staff plus a four-manned rowing boat. His job involved searching for smuggled goods in all vessels coming into the port. He shared the post with another Tide Surveyor, and the way they operated on a weekly basis was that one stayed in the office while the other was on the river.

The week on the river was the harder, for if an entire fleet arrived at once, the search went on right though the night. It was agreeable work in the summertime but quite unpleasant in a bleak winter of howling winds and turbulent tides. Nevertheless, from all contraband found, half of its value went to the Tide Surveyor.

In September, four weeks after reaching Liverpool, a letter came from George Whitefield saying he was coming to preach there the following week. The two men were delighted to meet again and, as it was John's week for the office, he spent each evening at George's lodgings, talking late into the night.

Liverpool didn't respond to the preacher, and he remarked that it was the most irreligious town he'd ever known. John went to hear every sermon and horrified his landlady one evening by asking her to go with him. She couldn't believe someone who preached on village greens, in fields, sheds, and markets could be a man of God. Under more persuasion she went, though, and was so moved she went to hear him the next evening, bought his book of sermons, and invited him, with four of his friends, to her home for dinner.

George was a regular visitor to John's lodgings after that, and the landlady appeared so spiritually moved, neighbors started calling her a Methodist— an offensive title at that time.

After more sermons, the townspeople, mostly from curiosity, went along to listen, and they too returned again and again until they were attending in the thousands. When George left for London at the end of the week, crowds followed his carriage to wish him goodbye.

After that, people were always stopping John in the street asking when the preacher would be returning to Liverpool.

In his next letter to Polly, he told her all George had said in his sermons, and it urged her to pray more earnestly. But, being so weak, Polly's aunt wrote her letters for her, and because the Catletts were *church* people she couldn't tell him the sermons had helped, lest her aunt convey it to her family.

Unexpectedly, though, she started to get better and soon left her sickbed. Before long she was going out of the house and her aunt took her to London for a short holiday. On the Sunday morning she went for a walk alone and paid a secret visit to Whitefield's Tabernacle. Now able to write her own letters, she told John it had done her more good than all the medicine she'd taken.

Some weeks later, Polly was so well she set off by stagecoach for Liverpool. How happy John was to be reunited with her and thanked God for her remarkable recovery. They rented a nice house in the town and invited George Whitefield to come and stay and preach again as people were clamoring for him.

This prompted John to write a pamphlet, *Thoughts on Religious Associations,* giving ideas on how to improve the spiritual life of the people of Liverpool. When it was printed he sent a copy to all the Dissenting chapels. Months later he produced a second similar paper for distribution to civic associations. Soon, John Newton's name was known all over the town.

A constant stream of friends went to their home where, on Sunday evenings, he held lighthearted prayer meetings and everybody sang hymns. Polly was once more her happy, fun-loving self whom everybody warmed to. The shock of John's collapse, however, had left her nerves in a fragile state and town life wasn't very good for her. For a break he took her for a long holiday into Yorkshire, a beautiful county of dales and wild moors.

There the evangelist movement was very strong and they attended several sermons given by various preachers. John recalled the times he'd told his mother he would one day stand in a pulpit of his own. If only he could, he thought.

Often, people at the prayer meetings were called on to testify of their faith to the congregation, but the first time John tried it his courage deserted him. He stood struggling for words that refused to come. Yet he above all could have made the strongest testimonial to Christ. The next time though, he was more confident. The third time, better still, until soon, at every meeting, he was being asked to stand and relate his incredible story.

Next he was being asked why he didn't become a minister himself, and even take holy orders in the church. Holy orders, thought John, a wretch like me?

16

Tribulations—and Triumph

For a long time John had sensed the Lord had plans for him other than a career in Customs and Excise. But why should He want a sinner like me? he wondered.

He began thinking seriously about going into the church and, hoping to find a solution, he dedicated all the daylight hours of his birthday to prayer, beginning at six o'clock in the morning. But by tea time, long before the hours of darkness, he knew where his future lay. He was going to resign from his work and be a Dissenting minister like his old friend, Dr. Jennings.

Despite what her family had said about Dissenters, once John's mind was made up, Polly gave him every encouragement—but then something happened to change his mind. He'd had reason to go to Yorkshire where he met up with a friend of George Whitefield's, Harry Crook, a Church of England vicar. And on hearing of John's intentions, the Reverend Crook immediately offered him a curacy in his own church.

John raced back to Liverpool to tell Polly, *adding* that it would mean a 75 percent drop in their

income. But she was so pleased that he was going
into the established church she didn't mind econo-
mizing and lowering their living standards, so John
accepted the offer. Before he could take holy orders
though, he needed to present character references
from three different clergymen.

The first three he approached refused on the
grounds he had Methodist friends. However, three
others supplied the necessary documents. Next he
needed to be ordained by a bishop and, as Liverpool
came under the Bishop of Chester's diocese, he
seemed the obvious one to ask. He was in London
at the time and likely to be there for some time, so
John traveled south to see him.

By coincidence, while in London, he bumped
into Polly's father and told him his news. Assuming
he was going into a Dissenter chapel, George Catlett was both upset and angry until John explained
it was a curacy in the Church of England. Then
George told him that Dr. Soan, the vicar at Rochester in Kent, was looking for a curate and offering
a much higher stipend than the one in Yorkshire.

John went straightaway to Rochester, saw Dr.
Soan and got the curacy. He then returned to London to be ordained, but the Bishop of Chester refused and merely added his name to the three character testimonials. Next he approached the
Archbishop of York. He even refused to see John let
alone ordain him because he hadn't had a university education. Not even the Archbishop of Canterbury would consider him.

When news of this got out everyone suspected it
was because of John's friendship with the evangelists. Religious reformers were viewed as a threat,

and one of their associates within the established church could cause disruption.

Liverpool people were immensely proud that their popular Tide Surveyor was about to take holy orders. So when they learned about the refusals, the whole city buzzed with indignation and the news traveled fast.

George Whitefield's colleague, John Wesley, asked him to be one of his traveling ministers, moving from town to town, village to village, but John refused. Although still a young man, he was beginning to feel twinges of rheumatic pain and was unfit to spend hours in the saddle in all kinds of weather.

A sympathetic Dissenter minister from Yorkshire offered him ordination, but John's heart was now set on a Church of England ministry. And if he wasn't considered suitable, then he would continue working for Customs and Excise.

As time slipped by, though, he grew desperate, so when an appointment in a Dissenter chapel at Warwickshire arose he would have grabbed the chance. But it was only a temporary post and he had his secure, *full-time* occupation to think of.

It was 1760 and, through various treaties, Britain, along with many other countries, was caught up in the "seven-year war" that had started four years earlier between Prussia and Austria. Because of the war, the volume of shipping coming into the Mersey was greatly reduced, so when he mentioned his opportunity to his employers, they granted John three months' leave.

Situated in the Midlands, about 100 miles north of London, Warwickshire is often called the "heart of England." The Dissenters' meetinghouse was in

Cow Lane, Warwick, which lies on the River Avon, about ten miles from Stratford, birthplace of William Shakespeare.

Both John and Polly fell in love with the yellow stone houses, surrounding lush farmland and orchards, and quickly settled down. The quiet soothed Polly's strained nerves, and John proved so popular that at the end of the twelve-week term the parishioners begged him to stay on permanently. However, he was only there on extended leave and returned to Liverpool while Polly went to Kent to see her family before traveling north.

Back in Liverpool the war was still taking its toll of merchant shipping, and there really wasn't enough work for two Tide Surveyors so John wrote to Polly of his dilemma. He wanted so much to be a minister, and if his only opportunity lay in Warwick, a place they both liked, then he thought he should take it.

When Polly told her family, they all wrote urging him not to. If he did, her brother Jack said, he would be despised by all true church people. He advised him to beware of pride; implying it was sheer vanity that spurred him on—a wish to be recognized as a minister rather than a genuine desire to serve God.

Polly vehemently defended her husband against Jack's allegations of pride and vanity. But she was inclined to agree with him on how church people felt toward Dissenter ministers. And, although she loved living at Warwick, in her next letter she begged John not to accept the offer.

At this, John sadly sent his refusal to the authorities in Warwick, then tried to put all thoughts of a ministry out of his mind. But it was useless. He was convinced the Lord had directed him toward the church—or chapel—for some particular reason. It was his vocation and he would never rest until it was fulfilled.

After another two years passed, friends suggested he establish his own meetinghouse in Liverpool similar to the one in Warwick. After all, they reminded him, every Sunday for years he had been holding prayer meetings in his own home. John was really attracted to this yet, again, his wife sensed he would regret it and advised him to think deeply before committing himself, all the while praying he would reject the idea.

Over the years, the Newtons had made lots of friends, from Yorkshire and Lancashire in the north to Warwickshire in the Midlands, London, and all the way down to the south coast of Kent. Two in particular were a Dissenting minister named Fawcett, and Thomas Haweiss, a Church of England vicar forced out of his church for being too friendly with the evangelists.

Letters passed between them regularly, and everyone admired John's beautiful handwriting, but most importantly, they asked for more stories. They were fascinated by John's early life. They admired his success as a slave trader and the way he'd endured and overcome harrowing ordeals. And they respected a man who was once godless yet now dedicated his life to the Lord.

The Earl of Dartmouth, himself an evangelist, had inherited a large part of Olney in Buckinghamshire, about 70 miles from London. And when a vacancy arose for a minister there, in an attempt to reinstate his friend, Thomas Haweiss, within the church, he offered it to him. But Thomas told him about John Newton, of his aspirations to go into the church, and suggested he give it to him instead.

At that very time, John was considering yet another appointment, this time in a Presbyterian chapel in Yorkshire, and was on the brink of accepting when the Olney offer arose. He remembered the barriers put up the last time he'd tried to take holy orders and reasoned that, being proposed by an earl, no bishop would refuse to ordain him.

Leaving Polly in Liverpool, he went the next day to London. Thomas had invited him to stay at his home, where he received a note from the Earl saying the Archbishop of York was holding private ordinations the following day. All candidates should present themselves at the Bishop of Lincoln's London palace for examination by his chaplain that very day.

As Olney was part of the Bishop's diocese, this seemed the ideal opportunity for John. Alas, he got the note exactly one hour after the examinations had started, which meant he had to run the mile and a half to the palace. He wasn't too late but was nevertheless kept waiting two hours before a secretary told him that, as they had heard all about the previous refusals, he wouldn't be considered.

John ran back, this time to the Earl of Dartmouth's home in St. James' Square to report what had happened. The Earl left his dinner to write a note addressed directly to the Archbishop and again John ran all the way to deliver it. This letter, however, bearing its noble seal and coat-of-arms, bypassed minions to be delivered straight into the

Archbishop's hand. He still declined to ordain John, but feeling he was genuine in his desire to enter the church, he thought the Bishop of Lincoln might.

John had many meetings with the Bishop, trying to convince him that he would concern himself solely with the tenet of the established church. He later told Polly it was as though he were being asked to choose between God and the devil. Why couldn't the established church understand that the evangelists also served the Lord?

Finally his sincerity was accepted. He proffered his resignation from Customs and Excise and, on April 29, 1764, at the age of 38, in the Bishop of Lincoln's palace, John was ordained Clerk of Holy Orders to the Church of England.

Although proud and delighted, Polly was a bit nonplussed at seeing her handsome, young husband clad in drab clerical clothes and feared he may become dour in himself. If anything, his sense of humor improved and he seemed to joke and laugh more than ever.

After nine years in Liverpool they were sad as they packed up and again when they said goodbye to all their friends. On the day of their departure, their send-off was equal to that when George Whitefield left the town.

It was May 26 when the Reverend and Mrs. John Newton moved into the house beside the church in Olney. It was a delightful, small market town on the River Ouse, and its church was surrounded by quaint, thatched cottages with large, flower-filled gardens. The townspeople were poor—dependent on farming for their livelihood while the women ran a lacemaking cottage industry. They weren't particularly religious, either, but John and Polly set about befriending them in a way they had never experienced from previous ministers.

In the days when clerics came mostly from the upper classes and were remote figures held in high esteem, John moved freely among his flock like a true shepherd. He visited their homes as any other friend or relative would and not merely in times of sickness or death as many ministers did. He only wore clerical clothes on Sunday for church and preferred to call on people wearing an old sea jacket and boots. In their homes he was the jolly sea captain who sat puffing on his long-stemmed churchwarden pipe while relating a wealth of adventure stories and making jokes.

In church, so many flocked to hear his simple sermons, that shortly after going to Olney he had to have a gallery built. In the days before Sunday school had ever been thought of, John set aside Thursday evenings for children and they came in droves. Included in the Earl of Dartmouth's inheritance was a mansion-house lying unoccupied for many years, so John asked if he might use one of the rooms for "his tender little lambs." And the man who had once debased the Bible stories now adapted them especially for children to understand. He also told them of his own childhood along with tales of the sea and jokes that made them roar with laughter. He gave prizes for good work and good attendance.

In addition to Sabbath services, one night a week he held a prayer meeting for adults in a neighbor's cottage. They too became so popular and overcrowded he had to ask permission to move into the

Grand Hall in the Earl's mansion-house.

Both John and Polly were so happy and settled that when a wealthy London parish became vacant only a matter of weeks after they went to Buckinghamshire, neither wanted to move.

17

The Pastor

Throughout the ages, there were always some people opposed to slavery. As early as 1688, in North America, the Quakers tried to establish a movement for its abolition. During the eighteenth century, the most outspoken in Britain were again the Quakers, who claimed it was immoral and disowned any member who owned slaves. As recently as 1755, the year after John left the trade, an Anglican bishop openly preached against it in the pulpit, yet few paid heed.

While some agreed in principle, if their very livelihood depended upon it, they were content to ignore their consciences. Others, eager for the import of tobacco, cotton, sugar—and its byproduct, rum—for their personal satisfaction, didn't give a thought to the slaves who produced the crops. Then there were those like John, actively involved in the trading of humans and genuinely believing they followed an honorable profession.

For some time, Thomas Haweiss and Alex Clunie, now retired from slavery, had been persuading John that his letters, giving accounts of his fascinating life, should be published in a book. But he'd always refused. They persisted, saying that the lurid details of his former life, his subsequent religious rebirth that led him to devoting his life to Christ and his recent ordination into the church would influence other sinners.

Finally he succumbed—on condition he could produce the book anonymously. And, in the August following his move to Olney, the book was published. Although it bore the incredibly ponderous title: "An Authentic Narrative of Some Remarkable and Interesting Particulars in the Life of —— Communicated, in a Series of Letters, to the Rev. T. Haweiss," within weeks of appearing in the shops, every copy was sold. Money from the sales came when it was most needed for, although the Newton's weren't affluent, they were always using their own money to help the townsfolk.

The book was effective in another way too. People from all over the country wrote asking John to help them in their search for God. One wealthy merchant, John Thornton, friend of the Earl of Dartmouth, promised to donate £200 every year for him to use in any way he chose. This, too, went to help Olney.

The greatest satisfaction came in a letter written by William Cowper, a thirty-three-year-old poet from Hunting in Cambridge, not far from Buckinghamshire. After reading John's book, he said he'd been inspired to write his own story. He was the orphan of a clerical family and had been adopted by an evangelist minister, Morley Unwin and his wife, Mary. He had a sad history of mental instability, including three suicide attempts and had spent a lot of time in asylums.

Sadly, just at the time the Newtons got to know William, his adoptive father, Morley, was killed in a riding accident. He and Mary Unwin were so distressed at this, they needed to get away from the district where it had happened as soon as possible. So the Newtons suggested they move to Olney where they took a cottage, Orchard Side, next door to them. They shared a huge garden and, living so close, were like one family.

Although Polly had no children of her own, there were times when she felt she had two mischievous boys on her hands. This was whenever William and John had been walking the highways and byways of Olney to return tired, muddy, and giggling. Ignoring all her pleas to get dry and warm, or to get something to eat or drink, they raced to their writing-desks to grab paper and hastily write down their latest compositions. Purely for fun rather than competition they vied with each other over who could write the most hymns in the shortest time.

In all, they wrote numerous ones that later came to be known as The Olney Hymns. Years later they were published, but not all of them stood the test of time as some were purely relevant to Olney, its people, farming, and lacemaking. The ones remaining are among the best loved, even today, with such titles as William Cowper's "God Moves in a Mysterious Way," "Oh, for a Closer Walk with God," "Hark, My Soul, It Is the Lord," "Jesus, Where'er Thy People Meet," and "Sometimes a Light Surprises the Christian While He Sings."

Among John's hymns were "Amazing Grace," "Spring," "How Sweet the Name of Jesus Sounds,"

"From Heaven on High," "Come My Soul, Thy Suit Prepare," "Glorious Things of Thee Are Spoken," "O Lord! Our Languid Souls Inspire" and "Be Still My Heart!"

One of Polly's brothers had been widowed and shortly afterward he too died, leaving a small daughter, Betsy, so Polly and John were happy to adopt her. Then a young niece, Elizabeth Cunningham, daughter of Polly's sister, was orphaned when both her parents died within a short space of time, so the Newtons adopted her also. From being a childless couple, and with William and Mary living so close, they were now a large and lively family but alas, Elizabeth wasn't a strong child and died while still very young.

While life, with its ups and downs, was going on in rural Olney, the voice against slavery was growing louder in the cities. At that time there were 14,000 black slaves living in Britain because whenever a planter retired or came home on leave, invariably his family brought their domestic slaves with them. Some were re-sold as "pets" for grand ladies—flunkeys dressed in satin breeches; others as lackeys to run alongside carriages as a symbol of their occupants high status.

One day a prominent young lawyer, Granville Sharp, came across an escaped slave in London. He was so shocked at the injuries that had been inflicted by the man's *owner*, instead of reporting him to the authorities he took him home with him to be nursed back to health. Later, he got him a job as a messenger, but within a year the African's former master saw him in the street and laid claim to him. And to prevent any further escape he sold him for

£30 to a planter who was about to sail to Jamaica. But Granville Sharp, having the weight of the law behind him, asked the Lord Mayor to intervene and got the African released.

From then on, Granville campaigned earnestly against the trade. And in 1772 it was decreed by the Lord Chief Justice that slavery no longer existed in the British Isles, for as soon as one set foot on British soil that slave automatically became a free man.

News of this was treated with mild indifference by the Reverend Newton at Olney. He disapproved as much as anyone against ill-treatment of slaves. But in slavery itself, he could see nothing wrong.

In January, 1773, William Cowper had another breakdown and tried to hang himself. Rather than allow him to be admitted to another mental institution, Polly insisted he stay at home where she and Mary spent the following nine months nursing him back to health.

During that period, John was quite unable to write any hymns and sadly, on his recovery, William never wrote another. He continued writing verse, though, and became one of England's best-known poets. John, on the other hand, resumed his hymn writing but only at the rate of one a week rather than one a day as before.

He still maintained his friendship with nonconformists and often went to their chapels while they, in turn, attended John's church services. Dissident ministers, however, could only go to his prayer meetings as they were forbidden to enter a Church of England church.

John was a prolific letter writer, spending hours each week on his correspondence. Occasionally he asked for some of his letters to be returned in order to compile a second book, *Candiphonia*, which was translated into three European languages and also sold well in America.

Among his regular correspondents were John Thornton's sister Hannah Wilberforce from London who, with her nephew and ward, eight-year-old William, frequently holidayed with the Newtons. Young William adored John and followed him everywhere, always asking for more stories and jokes, and he loved to be the first to hear the latest weekly hymn. Unfortunately, his mother, a devout Anglican, discovered that, although the Reverend John Newton was a Church of England minister, he also associated with evangelists. So, to protect her son from their bad influence, she removed him from his aunt's guardianship and took him home to Yorkshire.

Over the years, John was offered well-paid ministries up and down the country and, after George Whitefield's death in 1770, he was offered the presidency of his college in the state of Georgia in America. But the Newtons were content to stay at Olney for the rest of their days despite its overflowing river and streams, its mist and dampness.

Those conditions did nothing to improve John's rheumatism and the lumbago he'd begun suffering from. Polly always attributed them to his ill-treatment in Pey Ey's hands when he was starved, then later exposed to extreme heat, cold, and dampness on board Clow's shallop. As John got older, even on his daily calls, Polly fussed about, ensuring he was well wrapped against the cold.

They couldn't bear to be parted. Whenever circumstances made separation inevitable they wrote every day, with each one out in the road looking for the stagecoach bringing the precious letter. On the traveler's return, as the stagecoach drew to a halt and the door opened, whichever one had been away almost fell out into the other's waiting arms.

Although they adored Betsy, their one regret was having no children of their own, and John often thought wistfully of the little boy, William Wilberforce, whom he'd loved as a son. He'd lost all personal contact with him, but just as Elizabeth Catlett had done with him during his childhood, through William's uncle, John Thornton, and his aunt, Hannah Wilberforce, he was able to follow his progress.

He'd grown up to be a very popular young man in his wealthy social circle. He was a member of five exclusive London clubs. In society soirees and salons he was known for his mimicry, his joviality, and his singing. In the ballroom he was one of the most accomplished dancers.

All of these made John as proud as any father would be. If there was an element of disappointment in the boy's life, it was to hear he was also a gambler and, while coming from a devout Anglican family, he appeared to have little or no religion at all. Still, considering his own past and the fact that by then he would be no more than a faded memory from the boy's childhood, John reasoned he hadn't the right to criticize.

As the years progressed and John reached middle-age, sadly, he began to lose his influence with the people of Olney. Without realizing it, he had developed into the over-indulgent parent who spoils the children only to end up losing their love and respect.

He first noticed the change in October 1777, after a big fire broke out destroying row upon row of thatched cottages. Naturally, tending his flock, he rushed to give solace to the injured and worked diligently, finding shelter for the homeless. A month later, in the days leading up to November 5, recalling the recent disaster, he appealed to the organizing committee not to celebrate with their usual huge bonfires. Everyone agreed it would be wise and asked him to announce their decision from the pulpit the following Sunday.

But, determined to have their annual merrymaking, the entire township turned against John. They started thinking up reasons why they shouldn't listen to him and used his lifelong friendship with Dissenters as one of their excuses.

At ten o'clock on bonfire night a drunken crowd of about 50 revelers stormed through the town, shouting, breaking windows, and threatening anyone in their path. They made their way toward John's home and advanced along the road, chanting threats, and banging and clattering on improvised drums.

Always afraid of loud noises and sudden bangs, Polly started to tremble uncontrollably and Betsy was scared too. John was furious at seeing them so upset and prepared to go out to remonstrate with them, but Polly begged him not to. He argued that he'd dealt with ruffians many times in the past but she reminded him, in those days, on board ship, he wasn't fighting them alone. Now he was, and at the age of 52, was no longer a young man or a fit one.

Reason prevailed and, swallowing his pride, he went out and gave the leading rebel a shilling to go away and leave them in peace. Next day the troublemakers were shamefaced but it was no use. By then John realized, after fourteen years of caring, he'd lost their love and respect, and life at Olney could never be the same again. It seemed the tide had turned against the old sailor.

He ministered on for another three years, all the while hoping another ministry would turn up. When it did, it was through his friend, John Thornton. The church in question was St. Mary Woolnoth in the heart of London. Situated on Lombard Street, home to prominent city bankers and close to the Mansion House, official residence of the Lord Mayor, its congregation consisted of powerful, wealthy people.

Betsy didn't mind the change but Polly, now 51, had been gradually weaned from town life—Dartmouth, with its bustling naval dockyards, and Liverpool, which was growing daily into a vast cosmopolitan city. She desperately needed the peace of the countryside. After some searching they managed to find a comfortable house in Charles Square, Hoxton. Two miles from St. Mary Woolnoth Church on Lombard Street, it was in an area ringed by fields and woods.

Sadly, as they prepared to move from Olney, John removed the plaque he'd hung over the mantelpiece in his study when he first went there sixteen years earlier. Its inscription read: "Since thou wast precious in my sight thou hast been honorable/But thou shalt remember that thou wast a bondman in Egypt/and the Lord thy God redeemed thee."

It was 1780. John was 55. So many changes had taken place in his life since he was, if not a *bondman in Egypt*, certainly a *slave in Africa*. His raven hair had turned white. He had difficulty walking from the pain in his creaking joints. Sometimes he was barely able to rise from a chair, yet insisted on kneeling for prayers. Added to his infirmity, his eyesight, never good in his youth, was getting weaker.

Approaching old age, and believing his work for the Lord was nearly done, he accepted being "put out to grass" to live out his life quietly on Lombard Street. Though neither he or Polly knew—the most important years of his life were about to begin.

18

Soli Deo Gloria—
Give All the Glory to God

John's fame went before him to Lombard Street, so the parish increased in size as soon as he arrived. Some traveled miles to hear him—mostly people who had read his books and were curious to see the self-confessed sinner-turned-man-of-God.

With such a large congregation to care for, he made a practice of inviting people to leave notes on the vestry table requesting interviews with him when they could discuss their financial, emotional, or spiritual problems. These counselings weren't confined to the church either. He made his home an extension of the church and people flocked there to share their problems with both him and Polly. Poor people knocking on his door were never turned away empty-handed. Polly suspected some of them weren't genuinely destitute, but John couldn't believe he was being taken advantage of and was always ready, hand in pocket.

He started holding "breakfast parties" for young men planning to go into the clergy. Already overawed by the famous preacher and noted author, his guests were always apprehensive of his hospitality. They expected a humorless lecture from a dour, stern old man. But when John presided at table, he soon put them at ease, regaling them with hilarious accounts of his own first tentative footsteps into the clergy. So successful were these "breakfasts" that no one was in a hurry to leave him afterwards, and they usually ended up in his book-lined study, puffing away on their pipes until lunchtime.

Working in the city again, John was soon familiar with the escalation of public opinion against slavery. Every day the name of another group or individual was added to the list of people fighting against the trade—William Roscoe, Anthony Benezet, Thomas Clarkson, John Woolman.

Of course, for every one in favor of abolishing slavery there were hundreds in favor of keeping it. By that time, Liverpool boasted of having 50 slaving ships operating from her port, and the city was so magnificent it was said that any king in Europe would have been proud to have it as his capital. Alas, it was also said that every stone and brick of its buildings were "cemented with slaves' blood," meaning all the prosperity and grandeur was due entirely to the Triangular Trade.

Farmers in the west country around Bristol had made vast profits from growing horse beans; the staple diet of slaves in transit. Foundries in the northwest of England had prospered from forging handcuffs, shackles, manillas, iron masks, and "bit"-like contraptions; both of the latter designed to keep working slaves from eating any of the crops they were cultivating.

In John's trading days there had been nine fortresses along the Sierra Leone coast. By then there were 40. Abolition wasn't going to be brought about by small groups or individuals. Only an Act of Parliament could achieve that.

At last, John started to see slavery in its true light—an abhorrent exploitation of his fellow beings, God's own children. Within a short time he was filled with self-disgust that he'd ever participated in it and loudly condemned the trade at every given opportunity,

During meal times he would suddenly remember the stench of the ship's hold and the cries of the anguished, and his thoughts would make his stomach churn. At night his sleep was haunted by the specter of human beings put up for sale like some inanimate commodity. He recalled writing in his journal on board the *Duke of Argyle* how pleasant it would be to look back on those days. Now he prayed the Lord would *forgive* him for "those days," days *he* would never *forget*.

At the end of the service one Sunday morning in December 1775, a heavily clothed young man approached John and, fumbling inside his enveloping cloak, produced a letter which he thrust into the minister's hand, saying, "Sir, allow me to give you this. It is of great importance."

Without further explanation, he left the church, stepped out into the freezing cold air, and walked off along Lombard Street. At first John thought he'd been too late to deposit the note on the vestry table along with all the others, but the man's demeanor and words made him curious. Rather than open the letter along with the rest, he thrust it into his pocket until he reached home. On reading it, he was surprised, not only at its content—requesting a secret meeting with him to discuss some important issues—but at the writer's identity, William Wilberforce.

He hadn't recognized him and wouldn't have even without his concealing garments. It was sixteen years since they'd last met and as John was now 60, he quickly reckoned that William would be 26. The last he'd heard of him was five years earlier when he'd gone into Parliament as MP for Hull in Yorkshire.

Even more curious now, John immediately sent a reply inviting the young politician to his home the following Wednesday. Not wanting to attract attention, William again went on foot rather than in his carriage or a sedan chair.

On his arrival at Hoxton, his courage deserted him and, instead of going up to the house, he walked around and around Charles Square until he could summon enough nerve. Only etiquette prevented him from bolting, but finally he walked to the front door and tugged on the bell pull. Was he making a fool of himself? he wondered. What would the great man think of his proposals, when he must know how he enjoyed singing, dancing, drinking, and playing cards—albeit attending church regularly.

To William's surprise, instead of one of the maids, it was John Newton himself who opened the door and ushered him into his study. After polite enquiries about each other's health and what course their lives had taken over the past years,

William found the courage to tell John why he was there.

For years he'd been *seeking* something, some inner goal which kept evading him. Only recently he'd been reading the Bible and felt God was pointing out certain passages, such as, "Ask and it shall be given you, seek and ye shall find."

Now he was turning to his old friend for guidance. He knew the Lord had some plan for him. Should he give up politics, he asked, retreat from the world, and go into a monastery; become a recluse or give away all his worldly goods?

John was completely taken aback at these revelations. He'd always believed William was bereft of religion. He thought for a time, then advised him against making any of the moves he'd suggested. Surely he could do more good by being in Parliament than by being on the outside. There he had influence and power. As also in the case of his worldly goods, wealth, and social contacts. Carry on as normal for the present, he told him, and together they prayed that God's plan would soon reveal itself.

On William's subsequent visits to Hoxton, John turned to the topic that was increasingly at the fore of his mind—slavery. Instantly, William said he remembered standing at a quayside one day when he was about eleven years old and having a ship pointed out to him by an older youth. It was a slaver bound for America with a cargo of black men, women, and children in the holds.

Curious to know why, he was told they were slaves bought to be resold and forced to work for their masters on sugar or coffee plantations in the

New World. They would be whipped, starved, and generally so ill-treated some died, but that didn't matter—they were only slaves and more could be bought cheaply.

He had never heard of the slave trade and was horrified. For days he couldn't think of anything else, but being young, it soon drifted to the back of his mind. John well remembered telling young William stories about slavery but he'd evidently forgotten them.

While this was going through John's mind, William suddenly brightened up. He knew exactly what the Lord's plan was and that was why he'd been sent to John for advice. He was going to join the growing army against slavery. As a Member of Parliament and the fact that both he and William Pitt, the Prime Minister, had been at Cambridge University together and were now close friends, who could be in a more powerful situation?

With nine Quakers, he set about establishing The Abolitionist Society, and at the first opportunity he introduced the subject of antislavery into the House of Commons.

The wheels of power were set in motion. By 1784 the Consolidated Slave Law was passed for all British colonies, forbidding cruelty and harsh punishment. Working hours were restricted. Slaves were entitled to decent clothes, recreation, and regular meal times. Families had to be kept together, and any woman having given birth to six children was to be retired from work.

One MP, Sir William Dolben, on hearing a slave ship was anchored in the Thames, was rowed out to investigate for himself. Appalled at the conditions on board, he reported back to the Prime Minister what he had seen with his own eyes. As a result, a Private Bill was introduced to Parliament to ensure that ships may only carry the precise number of slaves in relation to tonnage—ship's size—and not as many as they could cram on like books on shelves.

In John's trading days there had been nine fortresses along the Sierra Leone coast. By then there were forty, and lots of shipowners and traders were resentful at the money they would lose by carrying less cargo. But surprisingly, most agreed and on June 30, 1788, the Bill passed through Parliament.

Later that year John had his autobiography *Thoughts Upon the African Slave Trade* published.

Prime Minister Pitt ordered a committee of the Privy Council to thoroughly investigate every aspect of the trade. And what more appropriate person was there to give evidence than the man proposed by the MP for Hull—the Reverend John Newton, of St. Mary Woolnoth Church on Lombard Street.

The bowed, white-bewigged little man who arrived by coach at St. James' Palace to give his firsthand experience bore no resemblance to the swaggering young slaver of yesteryear. And as he waited to be called, ironically he thanked God for sending him into the trade and for all those days spent on stinking ships. Without them he wouldn't have been in his present situation whereby he could help stamp out forever the evil trade.

In the words of his friend William Cowper's hymn, "The Lord works in mysterious ways." Looking back at the many coincidences in his life that

saved him for this day, he recalled the gamekeeper
at Avely who gave him a thrashing when transportation, hanging, or prison were the true penalties
for poaching; the tree branch that missed entering
his brain by inches; the time he was too late to go
on the rowing boat that sank on its way to see the
man-of-war; the letter from Elizabeth Catlett just
before leaving for Jamaica which drew him to Chatham where he met Polly; the way he got out of the
Royal Navy only hours before the *HMS Harwich*
sailed for the East Indies; the Englishman who
came to live on Clow's island and rescued him; how
his partner at Kittam stopped the very ship that
was searching for him; the miracle that kept the
Greyhound afloat; the longboat he should have been
on when it sank in the Sestro River; the flooded clay
pit he'd scrambled out of when others had drowned;
what should have been his new ship, *The Bee*, on
which the captain and nearly all the crew had died.

"The Reverend John Newton."

"The Reverend John Newton."

"The Reverend John Newton."

His name was echoing down the corridors from
one usher to the next, and he was being escorted
into the committee chamber where King George III
waited to hear his evidence. As the hobbling figure
approached, the Privy Council—five peers of the
realm and the Prime Minister of Great Britain—all
rose to their feet to greet him.

More wheels had been set in motion and it was
just a matter of time before slavery and all its ac-
companying horrors would be ended. It should have
been the happiest time of John's life—but he was
about to face the saddest.

Polly wasn't well and hadn't been for some weeks. She always seemed to have stomach pains but blamed it on nerves, especially when her John, now 63, and constantly in pain himself, was facing the ordeal of speaking to such an eminent gathering. But even after it was over, Polly's illness persisted until she was forced to see a doctor who, to her dismay, diagnosed cancer—a death sentence in those days. At the most, he gave her two years to live. She deteriorated rapidly and was soon confined to her bed. Just as he did during her long illness 38 years earlier, John spent hours sitting beside her, wondering what he would do without her but thanking God all the same for what they had shared.

Betsy was a wonderful nurse to both of them, and their many friends gave them every possible support. John had something else to be thankful for: His beloved Polly was spared the agonies associated with the disease in a time when powerful pain-killing drugs were unknown. On December 15, 1790, she took her last sad parting from her dear John and he was stunned with grief.

Nevertheless, he'd promised to preach at her funeral, for who knew her better?

Ten years passed, during which John devoted his ever-weakening energies to founding The Church Missionary Society, The London Missionary Society, and Bible societies worldwide.

In 1801, when he was 76, Betsy suddenly had a mental breakdown and was confined to the notorious Bethlehem Hospital—otherwise known as Bedlam. And although growing more and more feeble, John was determined to visit her daily. With his dimmed sight, he couldn't pick her out among the other patients, but whoever escorted him always waited until they were able to tell him she'd waved with her handkerchief. By yet one more miracle in his life, Betsy made a complete recovery, came home, and married shortly afterwards.

She and her husband lived with John. And William Wilberforce was never far from his side—his *son* and *daughter*, the two people he loved most.

He continued to preach but his sight was almost gone. He'd lost his hearing and his mind tended to wander. He was 81 when the nation held the Battle of Trafalgar's first anniversary services. And, against advice, he stumbled up into the pulpit to read the sermon but part way through his mind began to stray. He couldn't see and he couldn't find his way down the steps. That was the last time he preached,

On May 1, 1807, an Act of Parliament was passed making it illegal to ship slaves from any British territory.

On December 21, 1807, John Newton died.

On March 2, 1808, only a few weeks after his death, another Act of Parliament forbade the landing of slaves onto British territory.

This, of course, did nothing to relieve those already living in captivity. It took another twenty-six years for that to be fulfilled. In 1833, the Emancipation Act came into force and slavery was completely abolished throughout the British Empire. This came about in August, just one month after William Wilberforce died in July at the age of 74.

By the time the trade was abolished, fifteen million African men, women, and children had been sold as slaves, out of which nine million had died in transit to other countries.

One by one, other nations followed Britain, but it took more than a century to accomplish total abolition of slavery. And it wasn't until 1962 that it finally became illegal worldwide.

Epilogue

The eighteenth century has always been known as the Age of Reason, The Age of Enlightenment, and the Age of Elegance. Regarding the first two, there was little of either when it came to the suffering inflicted on slaves, and the latter—Elegance—came about chiefly from the vast profits made from that human misery.

Not until nearing the nineteenth century did people begin to look into their hearts and question the rights and wrongs of trading in human flesh.